Do One Thing

Do One Thing

The breakthrough you need for the progress you want

Dr Geraint Evans

Pearson

Harlow, England • London • New York • Boston • San Francisco • Toronto • Sydney
Dubai • Singapore • Hong Kong • Tokyo • Seoul • Taipei • New Delhi
Cape Town • São Paulo • Mexico City • Madrid • Amsterdam • Munich • Paris • Milan

PEARSON EDUCATION LIMITED
KAO Two
KAO Park
Harlow CM17 9SR
United Kingdom
Tel: +44 (0)1279 623623
Web: www.pearson.com/uk

First edition published 2021 (print and electronic)

ISBN: 978-1-292-33821-7 (print)
       978-1-292-33822-4 (PDF)
       978-1-292-33823-1 (ePub)

British Library Cataloguing-in-Publication Data
A catalogue record for the print edition is available from the British Library

Library of Congress Cataloging-in-Publication Data
Names: Evans, Geraint, author.
Title: Do one thing : the breakthrough you need for the progress you want / Dr Geraint Evans.
Description: First edition. | United Kingdom ; New York : Pearson, 2021. | Includes bibliographical references and index.
Identifiers: LCCN 2020044245 (print) | LCCN 2020044246 (ebook) | ISBN 9781292338217 (paperback) | ISBN 9781292338224 (pdf) | ISBN 9781292338231 (epub)
Subjects: LCSH: Self-actualization (Psychology) | Goal (Psychology)
Classification: LCC BF637.S4 E928 2021 (print) | LCC BF637.S4 (ebook) | DDC 158.1—dc23
LC record available at https://lccn.loc.gov/2020044245
LC ebook record available at https://lccn.loc.gov/2020044246

10 9 8 7 6 5 4 3 2 1
24 23 22 21 20

Cover design by Two Associates

Print edition typeset in 10/14 Charter ITC Pro by SPi Global
Printed by Ashford Colour Press Ltd, Gosport

NOTE THAT ANY PAGE CROSS REFERENCES REFER TO THE PRINT EDITION

Dedicated to my two ladies x

Contents

About the author

Photo by Pete Bartlett

Dr Geraint Evans (or 'G' as he is more commonly known) is an award-winning chief marketing officer and writer. After failing to become a rock star, actor or professional rugby player, he went on to hold numerous leadership roles for globally recognised brands.

Now a writer, speaker, advisor and researcher, he is dedicated to helping people achieve their personal and professional goals. Geraint is also a regular keynote speaker at a variety of international events and writes for the likes of *Entrepreneur* and *Forbes* magazines and the technology website *VentureBeat*.

You can find him on social media (@drgeraintevans) and at www.drgeraintevans.com

#doonething

Publisher's acknowledgements

———

13 **Roy T. Bennett:** Roy T. Bennett **17 LL Cool J:** LL Cool J **2 Mandy Hale:** Mandy Hale **12 Søren Kierkegaard:** Søren Kierkegaard **21 Eric Roth:** Eric Roth, The Curious Case of Benjamin Button Screenplay **26 Leo Tolstoy:** Leo Tolstoy **28 John Green:** John Green **31 Mark Twain:** Mark Twain **32 Booker T. Washington:** Booker T. Washington **38 Alvin Toffler:** Alvin Toffler **48 Walt Disney:** Walt Disney **54 Marcus Aurelius:** Marcus Aurelius **57 Oprah Winfrey:** Oprah Winfrey **57 Amy Poehler:** Amy Poehler **66 Jamie Paolinetti:** Jamie Paolinetti **68 Steve Jobs:** Steve Jobs **87 Marie Forleo:** Marie Forleo **94 Brian Tracy:** Brian Tracy **104 Samoa Joe:** Samoa Joe **107 Zig Ziglar:** Zig Ziglar **110 Tom Bilyeu:** Tom Bilyeu **115 Helena Rubinstein:** Helena Rubinstein **116 William H. McRaven:** William H. McRaven **118 Deepak Chopra:** Deepak Chopra **132 Michelle Obama:** Michelle Obama **144 Tai Lopez:** Tai Lopez **148 Warren Buffett:** Warren Buffett **149 Gary Keller:** Gary Keller **153 Penguin Random House:** Jeff Sutherland, Scrum: The Art of Doing Twice the Work in Half the Time **155 Dwight David Eisenhower:** Dwight David Eisenhower – an American army general and statesman who served as the 34th President of the United States from 1953 to 1961 **157 Thomas A. Edison:** Thomas A. Edison **158 Helen Keller:** Helen Keller **161 Zig Ziglar:** Zig Ziglar **166 Jason Mayden:** Jason Mayden

168 Mother Teresa: Mother Teresa **169 Jim Stovall:** Jim Stovall **169 Preston Smiles:** Preston Smiles **171 Patrick Lencioni:** Patrick Lencioni **172 Jin Kwon:** Jin Kwon **175 Napoleon Hill:** Napoleon Hill **9 Pete Bartlett:** Pete Bartlett

Preface – why read on?

How others have broken through this

'You never change your life until you step out of your comfort zone; change begins at the end of your comfort zone.'

Roy T. Bennett

First of all, thank you so much for buying – or borrowing – this text, or putting faith in the person who has given it to you by actually opening it up! If you've yet to buy it and are seeing if it looks like it might work for you or someone else as a gift – then great news, this is the introduction (and I'm hoping the text) for you.

If you are the type of person who doesn't often step out of their comfort zone and consider motivational books, then congratulations for taking this step into unchartered territory; if you are a self-help aficionado, then equally – welcome! I will endeavour to bring you a selection of new ideas to implement in your existing practice.

This text is designed to get you started so you can begin to feel you are getting closer to being the person you want to be and living the life you want to live. We all feel stuck sometimes. This can be a combination of many factors that, at best, are delaying you or, at worst, are blocking you from getting to your desired destination.

We'll work together to figure out practical strategies for addressing ruts in your daily routine, stress, a lack of communication or not knowing where to turn for inspiration.

After a difficult period in my life, I began to reflect on what had happened to me, my life and what I wanted to achieve – the first time I had ever really given myself the space, and the permission, to do so. I'm now back and firing on all cylinders after listening, reflecting and experimenting with implementing the various strategies, ideas and tactics that I summarise in this text. Now I want to share what I've learned to help you too.

What I'm not is another gazillionaire success story – you can find plenty of those on the shelf (or thumbnail!) next to this text if that's what you need to get yourself going. But I'm thinking you might be looking for something a little different. I'm just an ordinary guy: I grew up in a small, working-class, seaside town in Wales in the UK.

What I could not have anticipated while completing the final work on this text were the challenges that awaited all of us in 2020. Challenges which have invariably put strain on our lives, and in some cases caused loss, both personal and professional. My hope is that this text will serve as a positive starting place for you as we all adapt to, heal and recover from the events of this year.

To be clear up front before you venture in, there is no magic pill to take to solve being stuck – which might not be what you're expecting to read in a motivational text! But I hope you'll be the kind of person who appreciates honesty, and you know deep down that nothing comes for free and without hard work. So why read on?

What does this text do?

This text will give you a clear roadmap to achieving meaningful progress in your life, and aims to provide some practical ways to achieve the best version of yourself – your TARGET SELF. The text is designed to focus on gaining rapid progress over the next few weeks and months. It explores your thinking as to where you want to be heading in the future, but equally the focus will be to ensure you don't spend so long considering all the options that you don't actually *do* anything.

The various chapters will deal with my ideal of creating a 'target self' – a version of you in a year's time that this text will help you to achieve, step by step, in order to provide a demonstrable, but equally very achievable, step change in your life, and how you feel about it. Each letter of 'TARGET SELF' stands for a key theme in how you are going to do that – a step-by-step process for identifying what you need, what is stopping you getting there and how to deal with it.

In Chapter 1, we will cover the idea of 'T' as 'Time for you', and the vital importance of taking time for ourselves to reflect and plan – something that we frequently fail to do.

Chapter 2, 'A' – Address the past, will explore how to both own and 'unlearn' what you may believe about yourself based on your past.

Chapter 3, 'R' – Reboot yourself, gets you really started on your journey towards a new identity and an authentic vision of where you are trying to get to over the next year.

We tackle one of my favourite topics in Chapter 4, 'G' – Gain knowledge, where we develop some skills to be able to treat every day as an opportunity for a new learning experience.

Chapter 5, 'E' – Energy sources, discusses the essential need to gain help through positive 'energy sources' in your life.

Chapter 6, 'T' – Targets for this year, introduces my 'SIMPLE' objective-setting framework to help you set effective and measurable objectives for the coming year.

Chapter 7, 'S' – Sidetrackers, helps you consider reasons why you get knocked off course, and how to deal with them.

Chapter 8, 'E' – Everyday routines, helps you consider and implement a variety of daily practices to help provide a new structure to your progression.

Chapter 9, 'L' – Less is more, helps you recognise the more subtle things that are probably not helping you – as well as addressing the really hard concept of saying 'no' to all the complicated parts of life that will stop you progressing on your new course.

Chapter 10, 'F' – Focus and failure, deals with the need to continually balance a focus on developing sustained momentum, working in short sprints of activity, with, at the same time, an embracing of failure as a method of developing insights and a greater understanding of yourself.

I end the text, in Chapters 11 and 12, with some encouragement on being your best self on a daily basis and creating an exciting 'halo' effect to make both you and others feel you are truly changing and progressing towards being your 'target self'.

How to read it

Each chapter is deliberately designed to be a quick read – something you can do in 30 minutes. Or, if you're reading it on the road in shorter bursts, I've also broken each chapter up into separate step-by-step sections, so you can move through them at your own pace.

However, don't think we are going to take things slowly – on the contrary, we are going to learn how to do one thing that can be achieved quickly and repeated each day that will move you exponentially forward, if you stick to the process I'm suggesting. I know there are powerful lessons to learn.

So, if you are ready to get some new perspective, some support in perseverance to realise your ambitions for this year, and to hit the accelerator in your own life to make some positive change then great news – I'm going to tell you how to start doing that in the very first chapter – so read on!

Introduction

How others have broken through this

'Nobody is perfect, but life is about choices.'

LL Cool J

This text came about after a period of burn-out where I'd hit the very bottom of my energy reserves. In a weird way, it was only as it was enforced that I finally gave myself permission to take a period of rest, reflection and re-energising in my own life. Following a crazy couple of decades working, grinding and burning the candle on multiple ends, I decided to take a break, reset and reflect – taking the first ever 'sabbatical' in my working life. Since doing so I have managed to make some significant forward progress in my life.

I needed a break because I've had a pretty crazy career, with some incredible highs and rock-bottom lows. It has never been dull but, like many people, I found myself in my forties thinking 'How did I even get here?' following the first twenty-odd years of my career.

Without really seeing it creep up, I'd also reached rock-bottom in terms of energy levels and had pretty much burnt myself out – albeit in an often thoroughly enjoyable way, but it was exhausting me and was not sustainable. At this point in my life I was lucky enough to be traveling a lot as I was working in many different countries. This involved a lot of early morning flights, a lot of hotel stays and a lot of rushing back to try to attend family occasions. When I did make it back, I was not myself. I was tired, distracted and not being the father, husband or friend I knew I needed and wanted to be. I was burning both ends of the candle and the middle part as well!

What I didn't know at the time was that I was beginning to feel the cumulative effects of emotional and physical stress over a pro-longed period of time, which I'd been neatly bottling up and holding inside.

The tipping point for me was another evening lying in bed after a couple of flights and delays, exhausted but still somehow finding the energy to aimlessly scroll through Twitter before my eyes gave out (sound familiar?) and coming across what seemed to be a simple clickbait article promising to educate me on the 'Top 10 signs you are burnt out'. It read more like a list of things I was feeling rather than an insightful guide to health. I could see myself in at least nine out of the ten signs, and it wasn't until I entered the period of reflection that led to writing this text that I realised I had, in fact, been com-fortably ticking all ten signs for some time. I just wasn't seeing the warning signs, I guess. I realise now that I was committed to doing what I thought I needed to, but I was truly stuck on the proverbial hamster wheel – just step-repeating the same negative and dam-aging patterns. I also hadn't looked for, or taken, an opportunity to check in on how I really felt about myself. In reality, I was doing okay on the face of it, but not too far from the surface I was unwell, unhappy, not fit and not present for those I cared about most.

Now to be clear upfront, this text is not a woe-is-me tale. I am incredibly lucky to have the most amazing family, a great place to live and a little bit of money in the bank to afford myself a break. I know how fortunate I am to have these things, and while I never take them for granted, I'm now more than ever aware of being blessed. I also have come to the realisation that I need to do a lot more to share the benefits this blessing gives me in order to help others.

I know how lucky I was to be able to take this break from every-day life, with the support and understanding of my family and some downsizing on our outgoings to simpler and humbler things. I was taking some time for myself. And I was TERRIBLE at it.

Initially, taking this wonderful, life-affirming time off involved manically staring at my phone even more than usual and searching for a new job on a variety of mobile apps and instant alerts, designed to get me right back to what I was looking to take a break from.

I really was like Neo in *The Matrix* when he starts to learn kung fu and jumping between tall buildings – I just could not let go. At the time I was not sure why. My (former) crazy-manic-busy, jug-gling-spinning-plates-craziness of a persona seemed to really want me back to what I knew best. Taking time off was rapidly becoming more stressful than being really stressed and needing some time off. It wasn't all bad. We had booked a week in the sun in a few weeks' time and I was looking forward to it, but on a daily basis I was far from the many glossy idealised versions of reality on perfectly mani-cured Instagram feeds, or success-story-filled YouTube clips, of what a motivated person should be – i.e. jumping out of bed and high-fiv-ing the milk-person/post-person/Amazon delivery person on the way out to smashing a 10k run before breakfast.

I was still feeling a bit down one sunny Tuesday morning. I was walking home from getting a coffee after some random chore (which, in fairness, I now had time to actually do for once), and was thinking/ obsessing about getting another potential job, as per-usual, when a random thought crossed my mind – the kind of random thought that often occurred to me, but that I had not previously actively captured, written down or actioned. I thought – what would I tell someone in my position to do? I was really comfortable giving advice if I felt I could help people. I liked to do a bit of amateur coaching on occasion.

It was a simple idea really, and honestly that was the day the idea for this text started. What would I tell myself to do? First of all, ENJOY some time off where it makes sense for you. I know some of you reading this won't have the type of support system I had: rather than having a partner, you might be a single parent; or rather than having one job, you might be working four, and taking some weeks and months off may not be feasible. If this is the case, then you will need to do what you can manage to do – but some time off is better than nothing, and, by following some of the steps I'm suggesting, things will improve. Regardless of your circumstances, in the course of this text I'll offer creative ways for you to get some time back, even if you can't get away from all of your responsibilities and commitments, as I was lucky to be able to.

You might be thinking, as I would have had someone stuck this text under my nose back then, it is 1,000% easier to tell someone else what to do than to do it yourself. It is massively hard to take your own medicine. However, please come with me on this journey, as I am there for you to make it a bit easier.

I realised that I was pretty mindlessly working and living without any real purpose. I did not have a clear goal in mind, and was ultimately missing 'owning' where I was trying to get to – in fact, I did not even know where that was. I was not working towards a destination, and more importantly I did not know who I wanted to be – let alone making it sufficiently articulated and clear so it was not just a vague place, feeling or 'life', but something more substantial that I could really aim for. Key to this was understanding that it was also part of the journey to get there that really mattered, and that made it even more real. It became about my travel *and* my destination.

I realised I needed to develop a vision of where I wanted to get to, but also to plan (often very!) basic, foundational steps along the way. As with building a house, I had to imagine and design what the future *architecture* of my life would be. I now call this my 'target self' – who I'm trying to become. Okay, deep breath, I still struggle with how that sounds – but stop worrying if things sound cheesy, hyperbolic or just a teeny bit pretentious, as this is often the type of thinking that holds you back.

So, let's get you going. Let's form a basic plan for yourself, an idea of where you want to get to and who you want to be. Ready?

Sound familiar?

So why might you have arrived here, reading my text? Have you seen stuff like this before?

'Click on the link below for your daily inspiration.'

'Sign up and submit your email for 37 quotes that will change your life.'

'Follow me for more on how seven simple steps helped me to lead the life you want to lead.'

'Empower yourself. Be the person you want to be, need to be.'

'Take action today – create the successful life you've always dreamed of and begin to truly enjoy your life.'

You know what I'm talking about – motivational content designed to transform your life in a couple of clicks or a few minutes of video. You see it everywhere at the moment, and it's often calling you to (finally) make some changes in your life. If, like me, you honestly find it more than a little intimidating and, dare I say it, actually demotivating, it can create feelings of 'I'll never get there, so why bother'.

During my own reflection time I did a lot of soul searching, hoping to find some inspiration through reading, listening to and learning from a wide variety of sources – everyone from the aforementioned gazillionaires, to yogis, to productivity experts and influencers – on their thoughts, experiences and systems to help you achieve your dreams. I've listened to a lot of them before – you've probably listened to them too – but it's taken me some headspace to realise *why* they'd never quite kicked me into action before now.

I found that while a lot of the content and role models available are motivating, a lot of what they've achieved seems out of reach to normal people like you and me. Many of them come from a position of strength – endless riches, a perfect family life or a fresh start fully realised. They are also typically at the end of a journey many us would like to undertake, and seeing how good they've got it can be a little demotivating can't it? It is sometimes too distant from your daily reality.

Rather than feeling motivated, these sources often left me feeling flat – and flat-out intimidated by them and their stories. To be demotivated rather than feeling like I could take on the world when listening to these stories of adversity and how they overcame them is obviously not their intention, but I'm guessing I may not be alone in feeling a little cold. We end up watching rather than emulating them. This is what inspired me to write this text as I progressed along my own journey of self-development. I wanted to try to help other people set realistic and achievable goals in order to make some progress towards their ultimate destination.

In addition, I found with many motivational writers that their stories were all too often a summary – 'I, like, turned up, did some stuff, shouted, got intense and I was a billionaire'. I am writing this text because, if you are anything like me, you are often more than a bit intimidated and lost in that kind of aggressive sentiment, rather than encouraged. I also feel some of the books I've read over-focus on the result, rather than the process and enjoying the method of getting there – and, ultimately, what use are they if they don't help you get to the place you want to be?

The truth is that you can get to where they've got to, but it is going to take some planning and this has to come from having enough time to reflect, plan and then execute your own version of where you want to go. I'll take you through how I've handled going step by step to get closer to the person I would like to be – my 'target self', and your 'target self' now.

Other motivational gurus point to the fact that you aren't meditating at 5am, you don't have that mentor, there is no grand plan to where you are going, no 100k in the bank and no 10k run before breakfast. But, if you want it, all of these things are eminently achievable with the right practical planning, scheduling and daily focus – you just need to take it all step by step, and do one thing at a time. I want to move you from simply watching or reading about others' success, to *wanting* to change and starting to make that change yourself.

It was the idea of doing more of this reflection and beginning to deal with concepts such as journalling, meditation and how a person 'speaks' to themselves that really encouraged me to write this text. I felt, when reading a guru's routine and lifestyle, it all felt very distant from my own reality and the pressures of modern life. However, I also knew in my heart that not improving in these areas was holding me back from achieving what I wanted, so I knew I had to begin to recognise and develop my own positive and negative patterns of behaviour.

How this text works

I've written this text in a way that enables you to decide how best to use it, according to your preferred learning style or the amount of time you have available. It will cover a number of topics that can help you build up a new view on where you are trying to get to – as I call it, your 'target self'. Think of this as a rebooted version of yourself in a year's time – a v2.0 if you will, and one where you will have made significant progress in developing and applying new ideas that will help you design the future architecture of your life.

Each chapter contains a number of practical ideas to help you implement some relatively small changes that will have a big impact – including, for the sceptical or time-poor among you, a minimum suggestion to at least 'do one thing'!

In later chapters I'll take you through the next part of this journey – how I refocused myself, got out of the mental rut that was hanging over me since I took some time off, and how I began immersing myself in content just like this – books, podcasts, YouTube videos, chats and talking to mentors about how to progress towards the things you want to achieve.

Okay – so what next?

I believe, more than ever, that anyone can do just about anything they set their mind to, but I also believe that people are increasingly paralysed by 'how' to begin to take the baby steps on the start of their journey – and, if they are anything like me, struggle a lot more than the highly motivated success stories might suggest.

However, we all need to begin somewhere. As such, the twelve chapters of this text are fully intended to get you started on who you want to be and defining at least where you want to end on the first year of this new journey. I am hoping they can also be a jumping-off point for encouraging further learning and development of motivational practice in your life, to help you keep discovering and achieving your life goals, whatever they may be.

For those of you who like to write things down, I've included opportunities for you to to add your own key points and reflections, come up with your own actions and devise how you are going to break through on each point. That way, at the end, you'll have a number of action points we've developed together. I also promise that, if you get to the end, you will have a clearer idea on the direction you want the next year to take, and a vision for what your 'target self' is going to look like.

You will need to get comfortable with being more ambitious than you might normally be, but make sure this comes with being kind to yourself as well as others – both of which are mandatory for ongoing motivation in my experience – so that you are not setting yourself ridiculously unachievable goals.

How does that all sound? Are you ready to work through each of the above together?

You say 'So what now?', I say 'It is time to choose if you want to make some new choices – are you in or out?'

Great.

Still not convinced? If you want to get in touch with me I am on social media (@drgeraintevans) and you can message me at www. drgeraintevans.com

chapter 1

'T' – Time for you

How others have broken through this

'It's not selfish to love yourself, take care of yourself, and to make your happiness a priority. It's necessary.'

Mandy Hale

Ahhh. . . the thought of it. Time just for you. You. Just You. Time off from work, the family, the noise. It is funny how this notion sometimes sounds magic, but equally can create an unbelievable fear. Do you feel that way sometimes?

When it sounds magic, it is time away on a beach, or maybe it is a great staycation of bingeing Netflix on the couch. It's not always so simple though, is it? Juggling friends, family and logistics is fun, but stressful at the best of times. Sometimes, no matter the great times being had, different fears might creep in – maybe it's things like your impending return to work encroaching on the fun like a spectre in the background that you know is there, despite how enjoyable everything else is. I also often find that these times begin with a ramp-up of stress – massive last-minute cramming of work apparently so urgent, and so needing of your personal attention ('I could explain, but it's quicker if I do it myself'), all night and all morning before you catch that flight, or working when you are on that same vacation, or 'The Fear' (as my good friends Karl and Ben both call it – so it must really be a thing!) that you get the day before you go back to work, or first reopen the email inbox.

Either way, before you know it, the holiday is long gone, as are any positive effects it had. If you managed to do the total digital detox on this holiday, you've crammed it all back in since you got back, right? If you were anything like me, the promise you made to yourself not to instantly check every message and news feed on your phone the nanosecond you wake up has been broken. So now what?

Time away

My next step, after realising I needed to spend a bit of time sorting myself out, was to, well, book some time to try to begin to sort myself out. This, on paper, is pretty simple, but in figuring out how I was going to do it, I had a couple of realisations – I'd never done it before. Literally, I had never stopped and decided to consciously look at myself, review myself and decide on what bits I thought were going to work for me moving forward – alone.

Hang on, you might say, I have plenty of 'alone time' away from my family: I see my friends; I come to work each day for a very long time; I'm on a train two hours a day, every day; I go to the gym; I pop to the shops; I sometimes manage to steal 30 minutes to read the paper or watch some sports highlights, read an article or watch a quick video; and maybe even grab a beer. What else do you want me to do?

I'd say there's nothing wrong with these examples, but I'd also say this is not the same type of 'giving yourself time' I'm about to advocate you do as soon as possible. During these moments, we are more focused on grabbing respite, and if we do any reflection or processing, it's probably thinking back to specific incidents in the day, or worrying about a potential incident in the next one. We are not prioritising time with ourselves, about ourselves. Try not to let your mind wander to '. . . but I can't do that, it's not fair on X', or 'why bother?', or even 'I don't see why I need to do that'. Don't rationalise the 'why' yet, just book the time.

I appreciate that with an incredibly busy life this is hard to do, but, rather like calculus, it is probably hard to do because we rarely, or never, actually do it. We are not used to using our brains or our souls for that purpose. So, like the Green Cross Man said in the '70s TV advert (which at least two of you reading this will actually remember!), you need to stop, look and listen to yourself for a dedicated period of time.

So, your first action is both so easy to do and so hard to do –
but, hey, welcome to testing some new things. I'm right with you,
believe me – even though I thought about it, I managed to delay it
for well over a week, despite having very little to actually do with
my time!

Do one thing NOW

Your action is to book some time – depending on your personal
circumstances, this might mean at least two hours, a morning,
an afternoon, a whole day in the next ten days (so that might
give you two weekends to try and get it in). Choose a day and
time that is most logical for you – but you need to be able to get
away from your normal routine.

If you manage your own time, and assuming you don't have any
personal rules prohibiting you from doing so, as yet, stop reading
this text for a few minutes, open up the calendar app (c'mon, you are
checking your phone every 30 seconds anyway), or find your paper
diary, consult the calendar on the fridge or speak to (or email) your
partner asking for this time – not asking their permission, but simply
asking. You may have obligations or a lack of support that makes
this difficult, and I know that taking time away is not necessarily as
easy as I've suggested here. But do try to make time as best you can –
maybe pull in a favour you've been previously offered for someone
to cover you for even an hour or two to go and sit in a park or café. If
that's impossible, try to carve out some time early one morning, or
late evening. Again, I know this may not be easy for you, but please
do try to prioritise some time for yourself.

You can decide how to describe 'why' you need this time
(although please do give some element of reasoning – 'I'm going out
next Friday, can't tell you why, but see you Saturday' is not going to
inspire much trust and confidence), but book in a time like it's the

most important meeting you've ever had in your life. If you have relative flexibility on managing your own time, choose a time when you think you are normally 'at your best'. This can be different for different people – I've seen some come up with the best ideas ever on two hours' sleep, a terrible hangover or eating too much sugar – you know yourself (even if you've not recently reflected on where you are in your life), so set yourself up for success (as the gurus say) as best you can. If you are a morning person, consider setting an alarm, jumping out of bed and taking the steps I suggest next; equally, if you are a night owl, carve out an evening. In terms of 'where' – again, it is up to you, but I'd recommend going somewhere no one knows you or is likely to see you and therefore interrupt you. Perhaps it's somewhere inspirational, perhaps it's somewhere you know you'll get some peace and quiet, be alone and be able to focus with minimal or no distraction.

For what it's worth, I knew myself that if I tried to do this at home, I'd get distracted, so I literally did book half a day and drove to a hotel I'd previously stayed at, which had a nice outside seating area, and I sat there for four hours in the end.

Do one thing NOW

Please remember that taking some time to really focus on yourself for even just a few hours is not self-indulgence, it is self-care. I am sure many of you reading this have to consider others in taking time for yourself, and this can make things hard. Make sure you offer them the same option as well. Being open and honest about what you need can be surprisingly hard, but it is also a great first step on your journey.

Don't wait to do this. I appreciate that this may all be new to you. So consider using the following ideas as a guide and see how you get along.

Press reset

- -

You might be thinking. . .

You say: 'I just don't have the time.'

I say: 'You are not giving yourself permission to take time for yourself.'

- -

It is time to get more acquainted with yourself – but let's get back to basics.

Resetting is something that seems to be becoming less and less common in our life doesn't it? We put our TV, phones and tablets on stand-by, plugged in but rarely switched off. Apart from the old IT department joke of 'turn it off and on' if you have a problem, we also don't really encounter resetting in our life either, do we? With friends we check in and meet up, but things roll on – the same jokes come up, quick updates are given and on we go to the next thing. Same with work really – we don't often pause, or reset, on things – it is more of an ongoing dialogue.

Extending a bit further the analogy of turning your computer off and on, a reset is a fresh start but not starting from scratch. You still see a familiar screen when the computer comes on, a home-screen of options, but you can now choose to do something different with that screen.

Write down the first things that fly into your mind about yourself, and your life journey. There is no right or wrong here. This is you, your life, your history.

Next, ask yourself, what is missing from my life? Crucially, here I am suggesting you don't think of it as 'what would I change?'. Please, please don't get drawn into that line of thinking right now. I know you've heard it so many times before, but we can't change the past – that is not what we are trying to do here.

Instead, begin to think more tangibly: what kinds of things do you want to do more of as part of this change? New job, better job, better boss, meet the love your life, a supportive group of new friends or travel to the places you've always dreamed about? Again, it does not have to be overwhelmingly positive and rosy – you might instinctively feel you have some very tough decisions to make, hard things ahead. Just write some things down, as you did before, big and small. Where are you going next?

The next question, thinking about the things that are missing and given all the resources in the world, is what do you want to do first on your timeline in the next year or two?

Remember, you are not necessarily having to think about a complete 'rebuild' here, unless that is what you feel you need. So, by all means write down 'not been to Mars yet, want to go to Mars', but as even Elon Musk hasn't quite managed it yet, it might take you some time to get there!

Do one thing NOW

Start to write down (or say, or scream!) some of your thoughts on a fresh version of you. In the next chapter, we'll begin to plan these thoughts onto a proper timeline, but for now flip the page over and draw a new line, starting with today's date and ending in a hundred years (who wants to live forever?). Start putting down some of your thoughts – what do you want to look like in one, two, or three years' time? What will you have done in the next decade and beyond?

What do you want to do in the future? What are you hoping is no longer happening to you? What did you tell yourself when I suggested taking some time out? Do you still believe that person?

I've frequently stated there are no rules, but all I ask is, please, please, please, please put as much emphasis on positive growth and happiness in your future as you can. Life is really good at supplying us with a steady stream of negatives, disappointment and pain. I'd urge you not to put any more on yourself as you complete your future timeline.

Done? Quicker than you thought, right? Congratulations, you've just taken a bit of control of that future version of yourself and taken a huge step towards forming the 'target self' you want to become.

Give yourself permission to move forward

Now, before you can get to the rest of the work that I hope will deliver change to your life long term, one thing I quickly realised about my own future timeline was that I felt that I was not sure I could achieve this 'future' person. I'd failed before, why did I think I could do it now? My block here was all about permission, and for some of you it might be your block too.

We spend so much of our life seeking, waiting for or working based on permission, don't we? It's ingrained in us from an extremely early age. It's following the rules. Guess what, there are far fewer rules when it comes to your future self. There are not the same constraints on time, money, prospects – there is not the same two-hour commute (unless of course you like it and wish for it to continue!).

You now need to take a big step. Imagine your future self talking to you right now. What would they tell you not to worry about? What things, people and events have long gone away? What small details do you no longer need to sweat on? You know what they are. Who or what circumstances are holding you back from beginning a journey to becoming that person? Forget your background, what's expected of you (or not, if no one expected you to amount to anything) – forget everyone apart from yourself.

Do one thing NOW

Give yourself permission to improve your situation. Give yourself permission to recognise that you might not be exactly where you want to be right now. Give yourself permission to realise you've not achieved everything you wanted to. Give yourself permission to forgive and forget, if you can. Or, if you can't right now, give yourself permission to at least put those things in a box, on a shelf, in the 'will sort out later' pile in your spare room, and not let them block the way. Give yourself permission to achieve what you want.

Hard, isn't it? Make a note of the things that are still bothering you – things that some voice in your head is still telling you – but also write down the things you are totally done with. Thoughts, feelings and events that are no longer going to hold you back.

Steps to execute your plan every day

Just in case you skipped what I've suggested to do, you need to begin with doing the following this week:

Step	Things to do	Reflection and further builds
Step 1	Book and take some time off for yourself (no matter how hard it is to do that).	Think about where you can go to really be alone and have some time to think. When can you do it? Where will you go? Who can help you (even if it is really hard to take time away for family reasons)?
Step 2	Write down the first things that fly into your mind.	Once you have time to yourself, write down the first things that pop into your mind about yourself and your life.

Step	Things to do	Reflection and further builds
Step 3	Write down what is missing from your life currently.	If you really reflect, where are the gaps and what is missing from your life currently?
Step 4	Analyse all parts of your life in detail.	Write down what parts of your life you want to keep, do more of, or not do any more.
Step 5	Give yourself 'permission' to look into the future.	Give yourself 'permission' by writing down some notes on the future version of your 'target self' you want to strive to work towards.

Now, take a break – this has been a lot of hard work. Grab some food and drink some water.

How I personally broke through this

If you are still considering if this is the right thing for you, I understand and respect that. All I ask is that you do that first thing – book some time for yourself like it's the most important meeting of your life. Even if you can only spare an hour, even if you aren't ready to do the full timeline and projection thing, still take some time to yourself to reflect (and make sure you take some paper with you, just in case. . .).

If you want more

If this chapter has piqued your interest, you can find more resources, including videos and workbooks, at www.drgeraintevans.com

chapter 2

'A' – Address the past

How others have broken through this

'Life can only be understood backwards; but it must be lived forwards.'

Søren Kierkegaard

In this chapter I will encourage you to start the process of both owning and 'unlearning' what you may believe about yourself, encouraging you to embrace but also free yourself from the past. Ultimately, we need to learn from what has come before, but we also can't let it hold us back as we move into our future.

In this chapter we are going to continue the practical work, and build some more detail around the basic 'target self' you've developed in Chapter 1. We are going to create a detailed version of your past life 'timeline', and include key events (both negative and positive), people and experiences that feel most important to you. We are then going to create a future version of this timeline to help you begin to articulate the specific things you now want to see in your future, or to make it clear to yourself those you want to leave behind once and for all.

As I've mentioned a few times, I'm guessing this type of reflection and personal development is new to you. I know this might all be sounding and feeling a bit 'out there', but, trust me, this is a first major step towards improving the things in your life that you are not 100% happy with and achieving some big dreams. I have found that, for most of us, the things that hold us back are often tethered to moments in the past. However, like many things in terms of growing and moving forward, these are not cut and dried. A lot of the past is valuable to us. Learnings, memories, experiences can be both positive and negative for us – we just need to decide what we want to keep hold of, and what we want to lose.

Document your past timeline

The first thing to do is a simple exercise that rarely are we asked to do on a personal level – write down a timeline of your life to date. If you haven't done one for your life, then maybe you've done one for key points in a project or business plan. But, we are going to use this visual mechanism to depict how your life has progressed.

No, this is not original – I did not come up with this idea, and everyone does this a bit differently, so go with me on my suggestion as it was one of the key mechanics I utilised to really begin to progress on my journey.

When you are ready to sit down and do this, I suggest using mediums for capturing thoughts and notes that feel most comfortable and logical to you (however, do consider this a growth opportunity, and do things in a different way than you would usually!). For example, you might want to grab an A3 piece of paper and some Post-it Notes, or if you are predominately a computer/tablet user, create a new workbook. I'd also suggest having an audio recording device such as your phone on hand to record any thoughts that come to you during the process, or if you simply like to say some things out loud!

The first principle is draw a line across a piece of paper, and mark-up day zero (when you popped out!) to today. It does not need to be exact space-wise, but choose key events of the timeline of your life and put them in chronological order. Once you get going, it should look a bit like this:

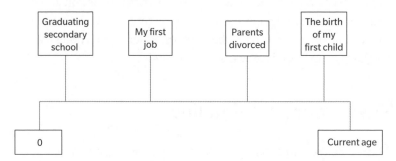

We need to be honest with ourselves – try not to just write down things that have gone super well and you are proud of. If something 'sticks' in your mind as negative, don't hide from it – in fact, you need to embrace it in order to move on from it. Remember, this is not a 'marked' exercise – there are no expectations to share with anyone else, unless of course you want to. This exercise is often done in pairs or groups during workshops and training, with the results shared and discussed. I'm all for open and positive dialogue, as we'll get into later in the text, but for me, I found to really get the most out of this exercise I had to do it alone, and to not self-censor from the off.

> ## Do one thing NOW
>
> It is really hard to get into thinking about the future if we don't come to terms with our past. By writing down our past, we can 'own' it – see it clearly and, to some extent, take the emotion out of it.

Think openly about things – where have you been, what have you done? Try to write it down as events as best as you can.

It's simple. Just do a timeline, just write it down – you know, a timeline. . . you might find this easy, hard, or maybe, if you are like me, impossible to do on a first attempt!

I know for some people this is a simple exercise, but for me it was extremely hard, so if it is for you, don't worry, I've been there – just try your best and make it personal to you. Persevere. As you go along, make separate notes (or on the same timeline, up to you – it is your time to yourself so no one else's rules here). Well done – you now have an incredible new asset to work with.

'Own' your past timeline

Okay, so next begin to really reflect on what you've done. What things were hard or easy to document? What things are sticking, making you pause for thought – both positive and negative – before you included them? Remember, don't censor yourself, don't think 'that's too small, that's too stupid to put on'. Also don't be afraid to recognise when something is 'big' to you – meaningful.

You might find a few things feel like what I call 'needles' in your brain – something, someone, or a memory you are stuck with that just remains in your brain like a fragment, not processed or filed away. These can often be uncomfortable, from friends who you feel may have wronged you, or a situation you found yourself in that you did not ask for.

If you found that process difficult, don't worry – I get it. It is so much harder to actually reflect on yourself than experts say it is. But the next step is simple – no need to light any candles or begin yogic flying (unless you want to!). Go through each of your events and give yourself some credit for the things you've achieved and permission to just 'let them be' if they are not things you are proud of or ever wanted. Right, you did that WAY too quickly, let's do it again!

If you are proud of something, really bask in it for a second – feel it and visualise that moment the pride hits you. We rarely, if ever, get the acknowledgement from others we feel we deserve or want, so a key skill to develop is the ability to give ourselves a bit of personal recognition and credit when we've smashed it.

Where you are not feeling so positive, do the same. Sit in it, feel it, but this time give yourself permission to not judge yourself too harshly. What did you learn from it that can help you move forward, no matter how painful it might be to recognise? Hopefully, some of these past events are feeling less like millstones now, and maybe are helping to sharpen your focus so you know what you don't want to repeat.

Doing my own timeline like this was honestly something I'd avoided in the past – in fact, I spent nearly six months on and off trying to do it, but doing exactly what I just suggested to you (and going back over it quite a few times until I connected with it for real). However, actually doing it became a key moment for me in my journey – both in terms of letting go of past events and experiences that were weighing me down, and (through the future timeline exercise) simultaneously allowing me to begin the process of hitting 'go' on the steps to move into a brighter future, because I was starting to see where it was that I was looking to get to! When I'd struggled to do it before, over time I realised I was struggling to face negative events and feelings, as well as the positive things. However, over time I learned that, by blocking it, I was essentially struggling to accept it was okay to prioritise thinking about myself, or that it was okay to explore the patterns of my past life to begin some level of detail for the future. So, if you are struggling with this level of introspection and have just skipped doing what I'm suggesting in this section, perhaps thinking 'I'll do that later'. . . stop. Do this one thing for me. I'm with you – no judgement. I literally could not do my own timeline for such a long time – I could not put pen to paper.

Part of it for me is that I'm naturally a very forward-facing person; I'm not too fond of looking back or being nostalgic (or so I told myself – we'll go into more on 'stories' you might be telling yourself later in this text). I guess somewhere deep-down inside I was not feeling proud of myself, or happy about anything I'd achieved really. A lot of victories felt a bit hollow. I felt I hadn't done enough even when things had gone well. I felt people were disappointed in me. *I* was disappointed in me. Despite doing some good stuff, I felt pretty worthless – in my mind.

However, when I (finally) articulated all of this on paper, something crazy happened – I realised that a lot of the negative aspects of the past where not as accurate as the 'feeling' I had about them. My mind was making it a lot bigger than it actually was in reality. As I began to put things down, step by step, there were so many memories that came up, people I'd forgotten and things I was actually proud of, and that were good to engage with. Of course, it was harder writing down the moments that had stuck in my mind as unsettling me – failures, rejections, death, disappointments – but as I did, I began to feel somewhat liberated from them. I mean, not totally – as I've said a few times, there is no 'magic' solution to anything – but it definitely helps to get things out of your mind and onto something else. So, let's do it!

Do one thing NOW

It is okay to not want to revisit the past for a variety of reasons, but we can't move into the future if we do not acknowledge its effect on us.

Give yourself permission to acknowledge that some aspects of your past may not have worked out 100% as you would have wanted, but also know that this is the experience that is going to let you move on with your life into an amazing new future.

I hope, as it was for me, that completing this task will give you a further spark of life – and maybe it is one of the first of many 'ah-ha' moments where you can change how you see something through a simple task. So, let's continue with the next step in the exercise, and get more connected to something you want to achieve next.

What does your future timeline look like?

Let's project into the future. First of all, close your eyes. (Yes for real, no one is looking at you, and if they are, don't worry – are they making a major change to their life right now, like you?) Next, imagine a 'future you', where just about anything is possible (and hey, if we can get to Mars soon, maybe anything *is* possible). Try to *feel* what this is like. What does this 'future you' look like? What sorts of things do you see, what and who is around you? Where are you? What is different from how life is at the moment? What is the same for you?

I know this is hard, and potentially you are already feeling a bit unsure about this. Maybe you are also ready to quit on this self-development stuff if it is going to involve projection. But, c'mon, you've taken this amount of time already – let's keep going.

Once you've formed your picture, at this point jot down some key things you observe about this person you see. Now shift your focus to be more analytical of them (yes, it's you, but it's not you yet, so go with me on this). Consider what their aspirations were as they went along the journey – what did they do to get there? This can and should be totally freeform if it helps you. Again, as with much of this text, there are no rules, apart from write down what YOU want, not what other people expect, and not what you expect other people want you to want.

Even if you are reading this ahead of taking your time for you, stop reading, close your eyes and begin to have a think about how this future version of you has come to be.

Got some ideas?

Right, now we are going to have a go at plotting them into a possible journey that this 'future' version of yourself might have gone through. Draw a future version of your timeline that begins where your other one left off. If you've used a really big bit of paper you can extend your past one, but a lot of people also like to start afresh, on a new bit of paper, to signify that the past is in the past.

Future timeline

For example, are you professionally qualified to do a future job? Have you done a course, a certification, got some key work experience? If yes, then plot this as a key achievement on the future timeline. Do you live somewhere different? What might you have had to do to get there? Saved up, bought/rented a new place? Moved to a different country? Again, put this down as an achievement. As this is heavyish work, I suggest you only plot into the future as far as feels comfortable for you right now.

If this is proving tough, and, as the majority of this text and the remaining suggestions will all be orientated around doing things to push you forward in the next year of focused effort, for now I'd suggest that you go at least five years into the future on your future timeline, to help establish some context to the journey you are about to begin in the next year.

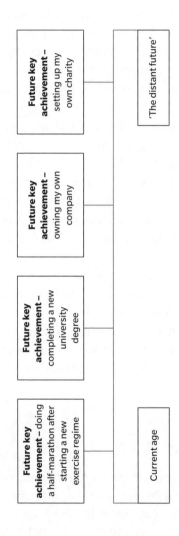

Just follow your feelings in your heart and your head and plot some things you know you want to have done or improved – or that you are just not satisfied with at the moment. Crucially, they need to be things you'd love to build towards achieving, such as a new job, a new home, to start (or grow) your own business, to undertake some form of new education, or even a new family member! I want these things to be inspiring or, if your mind goes to things such as 'get out of debt', things that will be hard but will prove to be a total game-changer for you. These future achievements don't all have to be personal – for example, you may wish to focus on helping others achieve their goals too. A lot of your objectives might be connected or interrelated to others – your spouse, partner, kids, family, work colleagues, employees. All of that is fine, but part of why I was so insistent on asking you to book the time for *yourself* to reflect on where *you* are and where *you* want to be is that I want you to start feeling comfortable prioritising *yourself* as well as others. Don't be afraid to want to do things for you, as well as for those nearest and dearest to you.

Try also not to hold back on bigger ambitions if you have them now. I'll say this time and time again, but it's absolutely essential: don't self-censor and limit what you feel you can achieve. As you put the future goals down, try to think sequentially – would they come in some form of logical order? Try to plot them step by step, building up into a series of events that will lead you to the end of this 'future timeline'.

Do one thing NOW

Draw up your future timeline. It is okay to dream about a future that might seem hard to get to right now. We can't move into the future if we do not acknowledge its effect on us.

Give yourself permission to recognise that the past may not have worked out 100% as you wanted, but you do still control your future!

What does your future feel like?

What is your future telling you? Is there lots to do? I am sure there is, but hopefully there are also some exciting aspirations on that timeline.

Look at the achievements listed, and your destination in whatever time horizon you've chosen – ask yourself, how does it make you feel? Content, happy, daunted? Maybe you see it more practically and words such as 'unachievable' are coming to mind. Anything it makes you feel is perfectly valid, because it is therefore succeeding as a task – it is making you feel something! When I did this for the first time it was really strange to actually connect feelings with practical goals – however, I've come to realise that this is absolutely essential to meaningful progress. I found, personally, I often 'took the emotion out of it' when considering goals and objectives. A lot of comparative exercises to this one actually encourage you to do just that – stick to the facts and coldly reflect. For me, this does not help you connect with *wanting* to do it. I realised I was potentially failing to achieve previous objectives for this very reason – I was not connecting enough with them, I was not getting fired up about them – it was all too abstract.

How others have broken through this

'For what it's worth: it's never too late or, in my case, too early to be whoever you want to be. There's no time limit, stop whenever you want. You can change or stay the same, there are no rules to this thing. We can make the best or the worst of it. I hope you make the best of it. And I hope you see things that startle you. I hope you feel things you never felt before. I hope you meet people with a different point of view. I hope you live a life you're proud of. If you find that you're not, I hope you have the courage to start all over again.'

Eric Roth, *The Curious Case of Benjamin Button* screenplay

So, look again at this future person who has achieved all of these things. How do they make you feel? REALLY feel – about the future, but also now. If it is easier then write down these feelings – don't hide from them, as they are things we are going to have to work on, or in some cases they may be the very reason you get to where you want to go. For example, if this future version of yourself is clearly a very determined person, then determination is a good feeling to 'own' right now. If you feel negatively towards this person – maybe even with words such as 'jealous' coming to mind – then, equally, you've got to deal with this as you go along, otherwise these types of feelings might morph into resentment as you progress.

Do one thing NOW

Reflect on where you are 'in the moment'. What are the nagging feelings you have about things you are doing that you know are not helping, or just could be more positive? 'Free' them (and yourself) by writing them down so you can begin to plan to tackle them.

The key here is to feel things, but also to know you can *change* these things – you can work on them and change your state of being. Let's think right now about some things you can do in the next year to get you moving towards this 'future you'.

Steps to execute your plan every day

Phew, that's a lot we've tackled already! A timeline of your past, a view of your future and a decent starting point for a list of practical things to change. Even if you've managed to put down just one idea, congratulations – you have now set off on your journey by starting with something most of us find incredibly hard to do – you've listened to your heart and your real internal voice.

Just in case you skipped what I've suggested in this chapter, here's a recap of what you need to begin to do this week:

Step	Things to do	Reflection and further builds
Step 1	Create a timeline of your life to date.	Once you have time to yourself, write down the first things that fly into your mind about yourself and your life.
Step 2	'Own' your timeline.	How does your timeline make you feel about your life so far?
Step 3	Create a new future timeline of where you want to be.	Write down what is missing from your life currently.
Step 4	Embrace how the future makes you feel.	Reflect on this emerging version of yourself and your life – how does it compare to where you are now and how does it make you feel at the moment?

Now, please take a break – this has been a lot of hard work. If you are reading this at night, time for some sleep; if during the day, grab some food and drink some water. In the next chapter we are going to look further into how you view yourself, and begin the process of 'rebooting' your mindset and focus.

How I personally broke through this

As much as I cringed at the time, I really did all of the things I'm suggesting in this chapter, and I really found them all incredibly hard to do. The main thing I realised was that I spent so much time worrying about what other people need, I never gave any focus to figuring out what *I* needed. I was always thinking, planning, coming up with new ideas, new schemes,

▶

doing new things, but I never paused and reflected on 'why' and 'where' I was going.

When I did begin to reflect on what had happened to me, my life and what I wanted to achieve, it was the first time I had ever really given myself the space, and the permission, to do so. All of the areas and ideas contained in this text all began with that moment as well – and I've been practising ever since!

In later chapters I'll take you through the next part of my journey – how I refocused myself, got out of the mental rut that was hanging over me since I took some time off, and how I began immersing myself in content just like this text – books, podcasts, YouTube videos, chats and talking to mentors about how to progress towards goals I wanted to achieve.

If you want more

If this chapter has piqued your interest, you can find more resources, including videos and workbooks, at www.drgeraintevans.com

chapter 3

'R' – Reboot yourself

> ## How others have broken through this
>
> 'Everyone thinks of changing the world, but no one thinks of changing himself.'
>
> Leo Tolstoy

How has it been so far? Easy, tough, motivating, daunting? All of the above? Don't worry, things are shortly to get clearer.

It is time to keep progressing, but now find a slightly evolved new persona for yourself (or confirm that you LOVE the current one). To make this something that sticks it needs to be an 'authentic vision' of where you are trying to get to in the long term, so you can begin to plan your first steps to getting there over the next year.

And there's no time like the present, so, let's get creating a detailed version of your 'target self' – remember, this needs to be a bright lighthouse beacon for who you want to become.

- -

You might be thinking. . .

You say: 'But. . . can I really be a different person?'

I say: 'Give yourself permission to become *yourself* as soon as possible.'

- -

What do you want to do in the future? Who is that future person? What will be no longer happening to you that is causing negativity for you now? I've frequently stated that there are very few rules holding you back. I know it is hard to see a way forward from here, or believe things can really change, but you need to begin with you. This might sound a bit 'out there', but it is essential you believe you can change. You don't need to think about this future version of yourself as someone different – they can be, but equally it can be about becoming a better version of yourself, your real self, a 'you' having fulfilled your undoubted potential. Put as much emphasis on positive growth and happiness in your future as you can.

So, your first action – wherever you are right now – is to close your eyes and imagine a 'future' you where just about anything is possible.

Do one thing NOW

Really allow yourself to imagine, feel and experience a future version of yourself with no barriers, no boundaries and no one telling you it's not possible. Spending even one minute of your life envisioning this will be a game changer.

Let's begin by embracing the thought that a future version of yourself could be quite different from the one you are right now – a 'target self'. Of course, usual caveats apply – it does not have to be that way and if you are happy with who you are, base the future you closely on this person. I am just encouraging you to 'let the shackles off' and really think big. 'Big' can be whatever you want it to be – personally, your character, the people around you, what you have and how you want to help other people (sorry, last one not optional).

Don't think about this person as your final destination, as such, but rather a key milestone – a version of you at a point in the future that feels far enough away that you recognise you'll need to evolve, learn and adapt to become, but who also feels tangible.

So, let's try really positively focusing on something: what does this future you look like? What sorts of things do you see, how do you feel, where are you? What is different from how life is at the moment? What is the same for you?

Next, think about the things that are missing – what do you want to do first on your timeline in the next year or two?

At this point, just write 'freeform' an initial page of notes (or tap them in your phone) – observations about this person you've seen. What are their aspirations? What did they do to get there? Just go with your feelings. Again, as with much of this text, there are no rules apart from writing down what *you* want, not what other people expect, and not what you expect other people want you to want. I'm trying to encourage you to tap into something deeper.

Now let's flesh out some details to give it even more life.

Who do you want to be?

In my experience, a lot of people want to be someone else but – and I don't think I can emphasise this enough – you don't need to be.

The phrase 'like a completely different person' is often used to describe someone who has radically altered their life or their personality – but they are still themselves.

It unfortunately does not often occur to onlookers that they might just have grown, changed and built themselves in such a way that it was hard to believe they weren't always like it. I'm pretty sure, though, that a lot of the qualities of these people were always there, just as they are in you. I prefer to think of this as wanting to be 'like' someone else, rather than becoming a different person. Even if you're not happy with yourself, you can change – you can get better in whatever way you want.

How others have broken through this

'What is the point of being alive if you don't at least try to do something remarkable?'

John Green

Rather than wanting to be someone else, I think it is more useful to think about our aspiration to change or be more like another person on a 'trait' level – think in terms of things you like in other people you like that you'd like to have more of!

The next part of this visioning exercise is to use this idea to think of people you are aware of – they could be family, friends, colleagues, or people in the wider world.

Ideally also think of people who have achieved *something* your 'target self' might have achieved as well. Don't censor these achievements. Think about it abstractly or specifically, whatever makes sense to you.

Consider why what they do makes you 'listen' to them and connect to them in some way. Is it their words that inspire others to action, or perhaps a common vision – a certain kind of empathy they have shown? An excellence in what they do?

Are they a committed person? A person who leads a team and never lets the team's feelings or efforts go unacknowledged? Maybe they are the kind of person who makes small but significant gestures of gratitude to people – to show that they matter and that their hard work pays off? Someone who knows how to say 'thanks' when others don't?

Maybe you will think of people who can present extremely clear and vibrant images of the future – a positive view of what can be achieved, but also one that is honest and realistic at the same time?

Maybe it is someone who is a team player first and foremost – someone who believes in the collective, a collegiate way of doing things for a greater good?

Maybe it is someone who listens, and then acts – someone who takes feedback on board and does something with it? This type of person might promote a clear and collaborative way of working, of leading. They will have a very direct communication style – they want to make sure that everyone is on board and moving forward.

Maybe you want to be someone who can express unwavering positivity – always to see the glass half full, and the bright side of some truly terrible situations, while all the time retaining an incredible empathy?

You might like people who seem trustworthy – someone who tells the truth, demonstrates integrity and does what they promise to do, or at the very least makes every effort to fulfil those promises.

Alternatively, they might be someone who just gets on with it, does things quietly without any plaudits.

Maybe it is someone who is genuine – seems real, seems to be exactly who they say they are?

Maybe you think of passionate people – people who inspire you by the strength of their will and belief? They are on a mission – either individually or as part of an organisation.

Maybe it is someone who is one of the 'best' at what they do – someone redefining a category, a discipline, a sport, a part of the creative arts such as music, books, movies or art?

Maybe it's based on their achievements – have they done things you want to do also? To surpass? To do 10% of, or 1,000% more?

Maybe it is someone with a kind of 'energy' that is hard to define but seems to seep out of their every pore?

Maybe it is someone who seems to have what you want to have? This is fine to think about – as always, don't censor. It can be totally material things – a house, a car, a lifestyle; or personal things – a family, friends, how they contribute.

They could be a celebrity, an entrepreneur, an artist, a humanitarian. For me, it is Oprah Winfrey who inspires me in so many ways. You choose the people who make most sense to you. It's entirely up to you.

Do one thing NOW

Write down a list of people you really admire (and a few you don't). Reflect on what they do and don't have in common – consider how you'd like to apply different aspects of who they are when becoming a 'new' version of yourself.

What do you want to have?

While we need to focus you on the future you in an emotional and characteristic sense, there are, of course, other elements of your 'target self' to consider.

It's okay to want things. It really is. It is a completely natural part of being a human today. Now use the ideas you've developed on 'who you want to be' in the future to inform this. What does *this* type of person have and what do they do with these ingredients?

Start making a list of what your future self would want. Private jets, tennis courts in the back garden and holidays to glamorous destinations are all fine if that feels right to you. You may want a nice (or nicer) place to live – and similarly a better car (or cars). Just as you thought about the people you admire (and don't), don't censor the more material possessions – just be honest about what attracts you. Done? Okay, park that for now.

Who are you with?

> ### How others have broken through this
>
> 'Keep away from people who try to belittle your ambitions. Small people always do that, but the really great make you feel that you, too, can become great.'
>
> Mark Twain

Let's address another important question: who are you *with* when you imagine this future version of yourself? Family – a new family? Friends old or new, or both? If you have work colleagues, who are you to them? What are you still learning from the people around you? What can they learn from you?

What kind of person do you want to be in relation to them? A good daughter/son, husband/wife/partner, uncle or auntie? A great grandparent?

As with the two steps we've taken already, in doing this visualisation it is incredibly important to listen to your heart and be honest about what you want.

What do you want to give?

How others have broken through this

'If you want to lift yourself up, lift up someone else.'

Booker T. Washington

Last, and absolutely not least, what do you want to be able to *give* in this future?

We've talked a lot about taking time for yourself in order to get clearer on potential destinations for your life, and any longer-term objectives. Assuming you've achieved them – no doubt through working very hard – what and to whom would you ideally be giving back? If you could wave a magic wand, what would be your long-term vision of serving and helping others?

Who are they? How do you want to help them? Reflect on the reasons you might choose a charity or cause that you are now giving to. Again, don't censor your imagination on this – think big. Do you want to cure a disease? Do you want to transform a region of the world? Or just help a handful of crucial people?

Write all of this down – get it out of your head onto a page or your laptop, and see how it feels.

Do one thing NOW

Giving something back to others is a crucial part of any future success. If might be hard to do this in the way you'd want right now, due to other priorities, but we can always give something back. While you are reflecting on more significant initiatives in the future, consider a small way you can begin to give back now to the same causes. Could you sacrifice the money for your nice mochaccino once a week, for example?

Reflect on these four parts of your 'target self'. Can you see any meaningful patterns? Do you feel you have sufficiently given yourself permission to 'become' that future version of yourself?

Remember you have already taken (and are continuing to take) a life-long journey of improvement and learning. I am sure you've had a lot of hard times, but I hope some fun while doing it. You've had your failures, you've had your successes, you've not always got what you wanted, but you've learnt. And now, having got this far, you are taking steps to change – so you CAN do this!

I feel we all need the use of a North Star when navigating the world. We need to know where we are headed, at least for now, and I hope the work we've done in this chapter feels like it's getting you closer to a clear view of your future 'target self'. I'd encourage you to continue to tweak this view, as you will continue to evolve your beliefs about yourself, to understand so much more about yourself. You will become clearer on what you stand for, what you value and what you believe. I'd encourage you to refer daily to this highly effective vision of yourself in order to provide a vision, a destination, a lighthouse beacon of where you want to build towards.

Do one thing NOW

When imagining your future 'target self', describe your future self in some simple sentences using this structure:

1. Who do you want to be? Start the sentence with 'I am now doing X, X and X, having achieved X'.

2. What do you want to have? Start the sentence with 'Through a lot of hard work and a little luck I now have X, X and X in my life'.

3. Who are you with? Start the sentence with 'Around me I have X, X and X'.

4. What do you want to give? Start your sentence with 'I am now able to give X to X, X and X'.

Read it back to yourself out loud (even if you have to whisper it!) and be sure you connect to it. Well done, this is a major beacon for you – a version of yourself to aim towards for as long as feels right, or until you do your next review. You can choose when this should be, but I'd recommend at least quarterly as you progress into your year of achievement.

So, great, you've now got the bones of a compelling future vision of a possible – and therefore target – version of yourself. Even more exciting, you've also got some milestones formed – some key achievements. But, ultimately, to get to even the first one, you (we!) are going to have to get used to executing things on a daily, weekly and monthly basis to get anywhere near these future ideas within the next year. Like the title of this text suggests – try to do one thing that will move you forward positively every day.

Steps to execute your plan every day

Thanks for taking the time to pause and reflect on the person you want to become (at least right now).

There is a specific reason why I did not get you to do this exercise early on. I wanted you to focus on movement, momentum and not getting lost, but now you've proved you can do it – you can change – then let's get going on this.

Perhaps you now want to consider some changes to your present work and objectives, based on this new 'target self'. Many of you will realise you are already on the path to becoming the person you want to be – your 'target self' is not so far away.

Step	Things to do	Reflection and further builds
Step 1	When thinking of your 'target self', think of who you are – start the sentence with 'I am. . . '.	Spend some time reflecting on who you want to be. What traits do you want to be known for?
Step 2	Think about what you have – start the sentence with 'Through hard work, I am lucky to have. . . '.	What possessions or freedoms are important to you in the future?
Step 3	Think about what you give to others – 'I am able to give. . . '.	How do you want to contribute to society? What would this look like?
Step 4	Think about who you are with – 'Around me I have. . . '.	Who are you with in the future? What energy do you have and need around you?

How I personally broke through this

Actually doing what I have recommended in this chapter was HARD. At different times it felt indulgent, hopeful, futile and hugely motivating. One thing that really helped me come up with a vision of my 'target self' was pulling together some inspirational visual representations of what I was picturing – some images of places I'd like to be, people I aspire to emulate, notes on key observations about myself and key quotes that resonate with me.

Some writers even suggest using these images to create a graphic collage – sometimes referred to as a 'vision board' – which you can put up on your wall or use as your computer desktop or smartphone home screen. You are then able to visually refer to something that is emblematic of the things you admire the most and that you aspire to form part of the future you want to create.

If you want more

If this chapter has piqued your interest, you can find more resources, including videos and workbooks, at www.drgeraintevans.com

chapter 4

'G' – Gain knowledge

> ## How others have broken through this
>
> 'The illiterate of the 21st century will not be those who cannot read and write, but those who cannot learn, unlearn, and relearn.'
>
> Alvin Toffler

So. . . your 'target self' is really coming together! The future version of you has some key characteristics, things you want to achieve longer term, good people around you and incredible new ways for you to give back.

In the coming chapters we are going to begin to focus more heavily on developing some key milestones that you wish to deliver in the next 12 months (to quit smoking, for example) that will underpin what you are looking to do long term, but also give you some fresh momentum. Talking of momentum, let's get going on something new now, shall we?

In order to prepare yourself for the future, you need to ensure you focus on the development of some core new strengths and capabilities. I'll aim to unlock some ideas in a structured and meaningful way through offering insight into how you might be suited to different learning styles, which might have been affecting your ability to learn to-date. I'll also propose some content to look at, in order for you to begin to immerse yourself in other people's ideas so that you can have an open mind and hear more ideas, thinking and perspectives to support your own growth. Sound alright? Awesome.

Everyday learning

Ultimately, I'd encourage you to begin to treat every day as a new learning experience. This might sound a bit simplistic – or maybe even a bit lofty. It is not intended to be that, but it is pretty straightforward in reality: even just trying to recognise and reflect on when you've significantly moved forward on something that was feeling like a big obstacle, or when you've finally cracked a concept or idea due to a 'breakthrough', will mean you have noticed something during each day.

- -

You might be thinking. . .

You say: 'Really, I hated school – learning. Do I have to? Is there a test?'

I say: 'Get excited that you don't know everything. You do know some things – but not everything.'

- -

One of the single biggest breakthroughs in my own learning over the course of getting my head straight, and in my early research of all of the areas this text focuses on, was appreciating what my own personal preferred learning style was, but also how I could use other styles to adopt the right learning strategy.

I find it truly amazing that we are not taught in school about learning styles – we have to conform to a specific standard adopted by the institution we attend. That was not controllable, but what is now is recognising how you learn best, so you can optimise your approach to doing just that – learning.

There are various learning styles available to you. It's not an 'and/or', it's about using the ones that make the most sense and, in some cases, combining them together to maximise the outcomes from the many different platforms and patterns available. As we've discussed at length, let go of what people might 'think' about your learning process – this is for you, and for your own benefit. You'll also hopefully begin to understand that this is a process.

I'd strongly encourage you to really begin to relish the challenge of learning and ENJOYING it, even if it feels really tough – this is the fun of personal development, honestly. As you are beginning to change your perspective about achieving greater growth and clarity in your life, this is also an incredible opportunity for you to improve yourself and your situation – so let's embrace it.

Remember, as well, that there are going to be significant twists and turns in the road – you'll go down some dead ends, you'll make some 'mistakes'. (But they aren't really 'failures', are they? It just means you are probably on the right track, but will need to make adjustments.) For now, the most important thing is focusing on the process of learning rather than the end result. This is tough stuff for a lot of us. These coming months will require a great deal of passion and perseverance to achieve your new 'target self'. All I ask, is that you push yourself, focus on growth, but please also be easy on yourself – it is an ongoing process. You don't need to learn by tomorrow everything you don't know already – you can take some time.

Next, let's investigate the best ways for you to learn. Interestingly, you've probably been working with a number of learning styles your whole life, from school onwards. You might well have developed a preferred style. When I started to understand this area in a bit more detail (yes, by learning!), I found that there are a number of approaches and classifications. One accessible 'jumping-off' point is the VARK model, which identifies four primary types of learners: visual, auditory, reading/writing and kinaesthetic. It is also sometimes known as VAKT (visual, auditory, kinaesthetic and tactile), and is based on 'modalities' – or channels – through which human expression takes place and which are composed of a combination of perception and memory.

Do one thing NOW

You are going to be making a lot of lists over the course of this text, and not just conventional to-do lists. One thing that has really worked for me is having one place where I put everything – rather than having multiple mechanisms for capturing 'to-dos'. (This idea is massively simple, and I must credit Anthony Robbins for it!) Try stopping having sticky notes, a notepad (or bullet journal) *and* your inbox – commit instead to trying one thing for a week, such as Evernote, Microsoft To Do or todoist (other organisation apps are available!), and see if you feel more organised.

Visual learning

While it's perhaps an obvious place to start, visual learners like to see things literally with their own eyes to begin to understand and learn a new concept. Visual learners generally also prefer to see new information in terms of mapping and connecting the relationships between ideas. To get a sense of if this is 'you' – think about how you react to not just written content such as books or magazines, but also to charts and graphics (such as those whizzy infographics you see). Do you like to see connections between points? If so, there is a reason!

Visual learners typically have two 'sub-channels' that they operate with – linguistic and spatial. People who learn on a visual–linguistic basis like to learn through seeing written language – so they are disposed towards reading, and writing tasks down. They then use this as a mechanism for 'remembering' what has been written down – it is concreted in the brain – even if they do not read it more than once thereafter. People who are more visual–spatial have some difficulty with written language, and learn better through the use of charts, videos and other visual stimulus materials.

Okay, so this is all very good and interesting, but how do you integrate this into your new learning? My advice (as always) is to keep it simple and go with your first instinct. If you know that you like to read and note things down, do that. If you know you react well to visual aids such as graphs, illustrations, infographics or charts, seek these out. Google (other search engines are available!) is an incredible resource for this – you'd be amazed what content people have taken the time to put into this format for you.

A bit of a watch-out for yourself in this growth period is to try as much as possible to eliminate potential distractions that may derail you – make sure you focus on digesting the content and making meaning of it. I also think it's useful to try to 'envision' the topic you are learning about in the form of a visual map.

Auditory learning

Auditory learners like to hear things as their preferred learning style. Interestingly, some researchers also believe auditory learners are more likely to talk to themselves and to read out loud. They also may have more difficulty with some reading and writing tasks. To apply this and see if you prefer this style, the world of podcasts and audio books is perfect for you! You might also find that, rather than noting things down physically, you do better recording them and listening back. This can be a powerful technique for emphasising key points. By saying information 'out loud', it might help you remember key points and also unlock new thinking as you are consuming it. Also, give yourself a lot of time to 'let things settle' and absorb content once you've consumed it. This will help you make connections, and consider what you can apply to current or future situations.

Do one thing NOW

As a practical first step, download a podcast app to your smartphone and start loading up episodes of different themes and content – you can also listen to YouTube in this form as well (or watch the video and/or subtitles if you are more of a visual learner!), if you prefer to keep things in one place (but do at least investigate the podcast store – there are some that are only there in audio format, and there is some really incredible content out there). I also suggest you take action to review this app every week, to remain topped up!

There are so many amazing podcasts out there, it's really unbelievable. From 'How I Built This' by Guy Raz, about how so many amazing companies have been formed and all of the lessons they have learned, to 'The Science Of Success' episodes, to 'The School Of Greatness' by Lewis Howes, to the 'Good Life Project' episodes – there are amazingly inspiring podcasters out there!

Learning through reading and writing

Again, not a shocker I'm sure, but people who prefer reading and writing. . . like to read and write when they learn! However, a key here to progressing is interacting with the text, as this is more powerful for this type of learner than hearing or seeing images. When making notes, as well as having free-associated thoughts, I'd also encourage you to focus on annotating key points – key takeaways that you can use in the future.

As an extension to this, if you like to read and write things down, continue to do so, but also challenge yourself to begin to develop 'maps' of concepts you are reading about, in order to begin to spot commonalities and patterns. Also, as you read, make a note of anything you read that is particularly useful or interesting, as this in itself can be a jumping-off point for further research.

Do one thing NOW

In terms of actions – this one you've already done by buying this text (congratulations!). But, do it more! What are you waiting for? Buy three more new books now from Amazon – and remember, when you get to bed, no smartphones allowed, only reading!

Kinaesthetic learning

This is the real get-going type of learning! Kinaesthetic learners are really motivated by getting 'hands-on', and are also seen as experiential in their learning style. These learners learn best by doing. So, in this sense, if you are trying to learn a new skill, maybe it is 'doing it' that will allow you to improve and connect with content or new things. Kinaesthetic learners like to touch and move, and also have two sub-types:

kinaesthetic (movement) and tactile (touch). According to some researchers, these learners also tend to lose concentration if they do not receive an input of external stimulation or movement. Interestingly, even when listening to lectures they may feel the need to take notes, just to be moving their hands!

When reading, these learners also like to scan material to get a 'big picture' first, and then re-focus in on the details. They also typically use tools, such as coloured highlighters, and take notes by drawing the information as pictures, diagrams or doodles.

I like to experiment with this type of learning by playing music while I'm reading, as it seems to help give it some momentum some-how! Also, please remember to give yourself a frequent brain break – I find it useful to spend some time just considering a visualisation of the complex tasks or new learning you are undertaking. Some researchers also suggest using stimuli such as scents or aromas – this may help you remember a topic.

In terms of action here, I suggest you use some of these ideas to experiment yourself and try new things – try using highlighter pens, trying 'doing stuff' to see if it clicks, etc. The key here is to seek out opportunities to actively challenge your learning style: if you generally prefer reading and writing, go to an event; if you only like to listen, try taking notes on what you are listening to.

Active listening

Another key way to learn is to develop better listening skills (even if you are a reader/writer, you still have to speak to people, after all), and while not a type of learning in itself, it is a great skill to develop as it will elicit more from conversations you have with mentors and people you meet who are experts in areas you are looking to grow in.

The concept of active listening is a skill that can definitely be acquired and developed through practice. However, it can be very difficult to master! It's a great way for you to focus on developing a new skill through learning, as the more you can extract from a conversation or audio/video content you may be consuming the better, right? However, like all good things, it will take time and some patience to develop. So, what is it? It is the concept of 'actively' listening – fully concentrating on what is being said by someone, rather than just passively 'hearing' what is being presented by the speaker. We should be aiming both to listen to and understand the messages of the speaker as a conscious decision. Key to this is also being 'seen' to be listening closely, and this interest should be conveyed back to the speaker by using verbal (words such as 'Yes' or even a 'Mmm hmm') and non-verbal (such as maintaining good eye contact, nodding, smiling, etc) messages. The by-product of this is that the person receiving this 'feedback' will typically feel more at ease and therefore communicate more openly and honestly. However, try not to interrupt with more substantive comments or words, as this can distract both of you and might place unnecessary emphasis on different parts of the message.

Do one thing NOW

As a listener, try to remain neutral and non-judgemental as you hear the content of any conversation – try not to form early opinions on the direction of where you think it is going as, ultimately, active listening is about patience. It is also totally okay to have pauses and short periods of silence – you both might need it, so please don't see this as 'awkward' and jump in.

Interested, active listening also allows the person you are interacting with the space to explore their own thoughts and feelings, which hopefully makes it more enjoyable for both of you – and hopefully more productive! As well as the verbal and non-verbal cues, also make sure to watch your posture. You may find that when being more attentive as a listener you tend to lean slightly forward or sideways while sitting, or you may do this with your head! Also try to use 'mirroring' and reflect the mannerisms and expressions used by the speaker – this is a great sign of attentive listening. Don't force it, however, as you need to be coming from an authentic place.

Also, please don't do anything rude – don't look at your phone, clock or watch, or do anything that would indicate you are not 100% invested in the conversation!

If it is someone that you'll be interacting with on a regular basis, then try to get into the habit of remembering a few key points about them and the conversation – ideally at least their name (obviously – but how often don't we do that!). Remembering key details, ideas and relevant concepts from the previous conversations can really help build a relationship that proves that your attention was kept, and is likely to be there this time as well.

During the conversation, you may not want to create forced interruptions but do make sure you ask questions. This helps demonstrate that you have been paying attention. Asking for clarification on what the speaker has said shows a genuine interest, and I think also helps you remember. Another way to experiment on this is reflecting on what you've heard through repeating, or paraphrasing, what the speaker has said to you to show you have understood. Building from this, summarisation – repeating a summary of what you believe has been said by the speaker – is a good technique as it allows you to repeat what has been said in your own words (hopefully baking it a bit more into your own brain), and by going through points in a logical and structured way, it also gives the speaker a chance to correct if necessary.

So, the action point on this is to *really* focus on key conversations you have – keep an (internal!) eye on your responses, your mannerisms, your body language. What do you do? Make a mental note of if and when your mind wanders and you struggle to maintain a level of 'active listening' focus. What is happening for you at this point? Do certain thoughts and feelings come up that take you away from what the other person is saying?

Also, recognise when you don't receive full engagement from someone else you are in conversation with – perhaps you need to amend your own body language and make it more positive in order to engage them further into the conversation.

Steps to execute your plan every day

> ## How others have broken through this
>
> 'The way to get started is to quit talking and begin doing.'
>
> Walt Disney

The key for me was learning that I was surprisingly 'auditory' in my learning style. My key to unlocking this area was a conscious decision to substitute about 50% of the music I was listening to for auditory help through podcasts and YouTube videos. This was me treating learning in the same way I had previously just listened to background music. One thing that really helped me was listening to YouTube videos – you can now do this with your phone locked, and also downloading content to the phone for later reference.

I also plan a week's worth of learning at a time, get it organised and have it ready to go whenever I get a second. Def Leppard can wait for a while! Depending on what you think might be your preferred learning style, consider the following steps to implement some of what we've gone through in this chapter, but do not see them as all being mandatory, obviously! If you are still not sure how you learn best, then you can also experiment with different ones to find out how you prefer to consume information!

Step	Things to do	Reflection and further builds
Step 1	Search for some visual stimulus on a key topic that is interesting to you to help you apply it in your learning and personal journey.	Subscribe to receive some regular content from the website, videos or people who have inspired you during this search.

Step	Things to do	Reflection and further builds
Step 2	Download a podcast app to your smartphone and start loading up on episodes of different themes and content.	Make sure you review your list every week to remain topped up – or find something new if it's not floating your boat.
Step 3	Buy three new books now from your favourite bookstore – now!	Enjoy – remember when you get to bed, no smartphones, only reading.
Step 4	Spend some time writing down your reflections on your journey so far – how are you feeling, what are you stuck on – what are you really enjoying exploring?	Reflect on how much you've learned – have you surprised yourself at how much you took in?
Step 5	Try to *really* focus on key conversations you are having, paying a lot of attention to how actively you listen.	Reflect on where your mind took you to. Why did you turn off at times – anxiety, disinterest, intimidation? What would you do differently next time?

How I personally broke through this

It's funny. I am a massive music fan, and I would use every single opportunity I got to plug in and tune out through music. I still do this a lot, but key for me to gain new knowledge was using times when I'd traditionally just listen to music to learn instead. Instead of putting on some hip hop as I tackled the cross trainer, I gradually forced myself to swap to podcasts, YouTube videos about motivational figures and audio books instead. As I sat in, or waited for, public transport, instead of flicking through a daily paper I'd have a book on hand to learn from. Doing this allowed me, and I hope you, to treat every day as a learning experience. Try it – honestly, you will be amazed how this helps you develop new strengths and capabilities.

If you want more

If this chapter has piqued your interest, you can find more resources, including videos and workbooks, at www.drgeraintevans.com

chapter 5

'E' – Energy sources

How others have broken through this

'Perfection of character is this: to live each day as if it were your last, without frenzy, without apathy, without pretence.'

Marcus Aurelius

Before we get into some detailed target setting, using my SIMPLE formula to set some stretching but now very achievable objectives, we need to clarify how you find the help to build on what you've started – through finding and actively drawing on positive 'energy sources' from people and life experiences, and (critically) by learning how to avoid negative impacts on your life. This chapter will tackle head on the difficulties in balancing family, friends, exercise, sleep and success, and will help you decide where it is logical for you to put your energies.

- -

You might be thinking. . .

You say: 'I thought you could not have it all?'

I say: 'Don't settle for 3 out of 5, or even 4 out of 5 – you need balance, and you need the right friends, the right family dynamics, exercise, sleep and you. You need you.'

- -

Balancing energy priorities

Life is really complicated at the best of times. Managing areas of life such as family, friends, exercise and sleep is the key to success in your professional life. It is pretty clear that these are areas that can invigorate you, but if we are *really* honest, they can also place a lot of additional stress on you. So, as you enter the days, weeks and months ahead of achieving the objectives that will help you become your 'target self', I recommend that you now begin to consciously decide where you want to put your energy during this period.

You might be thinking – whatever, I'll skip this chapter. It's easy, right? You'll juggle all of it as normal, right? Hmmm, it's not that easy though is it? In fact, it is often a hidden way we get derailed.

Endless ink (and pixel space) has been spent discussing the challenges of work–life balance for company founders, business leaders and high performers. Such is the stretch that general life creates for you, many entrepreneurial experts (or at least those who think they are experts) have extensively covered the fact that they feel it is basically impossible to do everything with any quality.

In fact, there are some, such as Randi Zuckerberg (entrepreneur and former director of market development at Facebook – and, yes, Mark Zuckerberg's sister) who write of the 'entrepreneur's dilemma', and who strongly suggest that the key to success is the need for anyone (and therefore you) to focus on only three out of friends, family, exercise and sleep in order to build a successful company.

In fairness, in her summary, Randi Zuckerberg was trying to convey the challenges and trade-offs of the entrepreneurial lifestyle. Here is how she puts the options:

1 Maintaining friendships

2 Spending time with family

3 Staying fit

4 Getting sleep

5 Building a great company

Randi suggests you must only pick only three of these and essentially 'forget the rest' in order to really get ahead. I totally get the intention here (less is more, really focus) – all of the things we've talked about at length so far in this text.

Honestly, though, for the vast majority of people I personally don't agree with this position at all, in case you are already getting nervous! I don't agree with it at all. It is my honest belief that to be a happy, rounded and successful human being it is crucial to balance *all* of these things, not exclude any of them. I totally get the principle she is trying to get over – about focus, about sacrifice – which is totally understandable. However, I think a life without even one of the five things listed is limited in its potential.

As a build on this list, I'd also throw in 'alone time' as well, but this takes preparedness, a strong will and constant organisation. I think one thing that is useful about this dialogue is that you do need to make a conscious decision on where you want to focus your energy, or if you decide (as I honestly did) to go against the grain and focus on all five things. If in your heart you feel you can't let any of these go, then I advocate that you need to begin to develop new behaviours in order to use them.

In this way I believe they can all combine to truly energise you, and you can use them to help begin to deliver on your commitments to yourself in your end-state vision. I'm assuming that many of your 'target self' personal visions relate to business objectives, so I'm not going to debate here the need to 'focus' on your business, or what you want to achieve in your personal life this coming year. For me, this is a given – and we've already agreed that you are going to adopt a new routine to your day (or night) to deliver things. Later chapters will help you turbocharge this.

You will also need to decide where you want to put your energy when you are not trying to achieve these things. However, before we get into the different options, and opportunities, there are a couple of key things to bear in mind, no matter what route you choose. You are going to need to be flexible. Flexibility is key to adapt to what is going on, and to not be reactive, or worse upset, if things don't go exactly the way you expected or planned. Also, be mindful of your own personal confidence – be confident in what you are trying to do, trust that things will work out and get ready to not be shaken if any of the things we'll discuss here destabilise that. We've already talked about the importance of cheerfulness and being positive, but as well as focusing on transmitting that, also try to focus on demonstrating a high level of energy and vitality in all of your engagements.

Cultivate friendship energy

How others have broken through this

'Surround yourself with only people who are going to lift you higher.'

Oprah Winfrey

'Find a group of people who challenge and inspire you, spend a lot of time with them, and it will change your life.'

Amy Poehler

Friendships are a funny thing, aren't they? They come and go in life. Sometimes things and people drift apart, sometimes it's a little more sudden and difficult. The importance of whom you associate with in your free time is the topic of many a podcast and evangelical entrepreneur rant. A lot of this concerns the debate about surrounding yourself with people who are additive to your life and your 'target self' personal vision. Jim Rohn says you are the 'average of the five [people] you spend the most time with' – fascinating idea really. Do you really feel like that? Another interesting debate here is the extent to which you benchmark yourself against your friends in the first place. I think, if we are being honest, we do. We may not do it in a judgemental way, but I think it's natural to look at the aspects of life that are often the most material, such as cars, houses, jobs, etc. This has a lot of pros and cons that are pretty obvious – it's worth thinking about why and what it is you feel you lack or have 'above them', but for me the more interesting exercise is connected to the theme of this chapter – energy. I guess we don't really think about our friends' energy as often as we think about what they have. Why is this?

According to some of the entrepreneurial gurus, growing into the successful person you wish to be is predicated on mixing with people you aspire to be from a business perspective.

For me, all I'd ask is that you reflect on those friends you see most regularly – let's take the top five we mentioned previously. What I think is essential is to reflect on what they give you in terms of positivity. Do you feel they don't take you seriously? Would you feel comfortable sharing with them your trials and tribulations? Do you feel you can talk about yourself without them just waiting for an opportunity to talk about themselves instead?

Talking is going to be so important to your process over the coming year. Talking and sharing. The old clichés are sometimes there for a good reason – you know 'a problem shared. . . ' and all that. But, wow! What a difference it makes to have people who can help you and listen to you during this process.

We'll talk about how to handle the negative 'splinters' in your mind in the coming chapters, but if you use friends correctly, they will help support the positive action in your mind. This will take some trust, of course, and also some organisation.

Do one thing NOW

You need to actively choose your friendships – they are one of the few things you 'can' have control over. Really reflect on whether you are getting what you are looking for, and if it's equal to what you are putting in.

I literally now have a list (yes, you know I love my lists!) of friends who I ensure I keep up with on a regular basis. It is not super-formally timetabled, but I just check it now and again on a flight or a train journey where it is not so practical to do substantial work. I also then use an app such as WhatsApp to send a bunch of messages – checking in and suggesting a meet up soon. Sure, I have other friends and acquaintances I see far more seldomly, and I'll occasionally do the same reach-out to them.

If you decide to end a friendship that is not positive, try not to burn any bridges, but make sure you do what you feel is right for you. This is of course easier said than done. Be nice, considerate, but be firm. Try to slowly phase out the things you commonly did with them previously – whether that was in person or in the form of responding to messages on your phone. Try to see them less, respond less and reassess how you feel as you go along.

Cultivate family energy

Family is a loaded topic at the best of times: I could spend the whole of this text on the psychological complexity it represents. All I would say is that, as with the analysis of your friends, choose when, where and with whom you want to expend your energy.

Do one thing NOW

A connected point here is that when you are with your family, be WITH your family. Do not stare at your smartphone to check for messages. Try to do non-digital stuff with them whenever you can – instead of always watching a movie, go for a walk, go to the park. Actually spend time and connect with them, rather than just giving them your partial attention.

I am conscious that you can over-schedule, but I'd really encourage you to consider actively (at least more actively than waking up on a Saturday and saying 'what shall we do today?') what you are going to do in your family time. We all need the days where we do very little, but try to make sure you've got some where you do a lot! Plan trips to attractions, the parks you've been meaning to go to, special events, the movies – there is always something to do. You just need to plan it in, like everything else in your life. This will also help provide space for you to proactively plan the execution of your 'target self' personal vision.

Cultivate exercise energy

WOW! WOW! WOW! Does this make all the difference! All of my adult life I've been battling twenty pounds for ownership of my midriff and hips. Sometimes I'm winning. And it's so weird – when I watch what I drink and eat and do a bit more exercise, I start winning in so many other areas of my life too. There are plenty of opportunities to embrace exercise in your life. With YouTube videos being so good, it's also more possible than ever to work out at home if you don't feel comfortable going to a gym or boot-camp session.

Do one thing NOW

Whether walking, running or using kettlebells is your thing, I'd massively recommend using exercise as a time to listen to the podcasts you've got saved up, rather than just defaulting to listening to the same old music. This includes using the time for getting ready and cooling down/stretching – it's a massive time window to really apply some of the principles of learning new knowledge that we explored in Chapter 4.

As with so much of this text, think about what works best as part of your daily routine, and build it in so that you *can* do it – rather than having an excuse to avoid completing it by delaying it or putting it off to another day!

Cultivate sleep energy

It is amazing, for something so absolutely essential to our lives as sleep, how relatively little focus we give it, and rarely 'plan it' either. Addressing this could be a total game-changer for you.

A number of writers talk about the importance of structured sleep. I know there was a fad for a while that followed the 'I need four hours of sleep each night to be productive' school of thinking. Other writers suggest a fixed time (within reason, you've got to let your hair down sometimes!) for going to bed and a fixed time for getting up. As we discussed previously, this might aid adopting a structured start to the day.

The key here in terms of 'cultivating' sleep is to do exactly that – treat it as something you *need* to do, not something that you just do, if that makes sense? Are you a night owl? If so, does it make sense to do more towards achieving your goal in the evening, so that you can sleep in a little later the next morning? If (like me) you like to go to bed early, could you go even earlier and get up a bit earlier to start working on your action plan?

This is probably as good a time as any to also address the dreaded 'snooze button' debate. It is clear that many motivators major on the 'not hitting the snooze button' in the morning. Honestly, I've gone back and forth on this, but I have found it be effective to adopt a strategy towards it as part of a structured sleep routine. For what it's worth, I also find the 'snooze button' becomes something of a non-issue if you get the right amount of sleep for you – it feels a little easier to not hit it if you are sufficiently rested.

Do one thing NOW

Start to think of sleep as one of the most important things to plan and execute each day. Stop watching box sets until you fall asleep, or endlessly scrolling through social media and/or work emails on your phone. The 'blue light' from your smartphone is disruptive in terms of helping you get to sleep – and don't worry, it will all still be there in the morning! Instead, think about how much sleep you need in order to be ready for tomorrow.

If you are finding it hard to break the snooze habit, try the Mel Robbins five-second-rule technique (see Chapter 7), or try putting the phone in a part of your bedroom where you need to get up physically to turn off the snooze alarm – at least you'll be out of bed then! It's harder to go back to sleep at that point, and if you risk disturbing your partner then it's even more of an incentive to get to the phone quick and turn it off!

The main thing is to plan and execute your sleep in a thoughtful way. Don't just let it happen by chance!

Cultivate me time

Do I need to spell this one out for you? Isn't it amazing how seldom we actually do anything for ourselves in this crazy world of ours?

To some extent this whole text is about cultivating 'you', but I don't think there is any harm in getting you to ponder this specific point as you read this. One element that I think is critical is to be kind to yourself. Call it what you want – me time, chill-out time, special time – you need it. The biggest mistake I feel you can make here is trying to be a hero and prioritising everything above this, and never getting to it. Treat finding time for yourself as you would planning and prioritising everything else in this new life of yours.

This time might look like a lot of different things – from a night away in a hotel to clear your mind, to perhaps booking some time with someone to help unlock or treat something you've been putting off – a physiotherapist, an osteopath, a massage therapist, a visit to the doctor.

Sometimes, no matter what I've done to relax, get support or tune out, I do still have feelings that hang around – some kind of negativity I can't shake. You'll find, hopefully, that over time, with more focus on progressing towards tasks and achievements, that these feelings will diminish. But we are human, so they are going to come up from time to time.

Mental health matters. You need to get your head around this, and a good way to do that is to find techniques that force you to become aware of your self-destruct pattern. You can't stop yourself spiralling a little out of control sometimes, but you don't want full self-destruct.

Steps to execute your plan every day

I have found actively thinking about the things in this chapter as a very strange thing to do. I'd never sat down before and considered where I was putting my energy, and if I should look to prioritise it. The other major outcome for me was a realisation that often I was actually doing the opposite of what I was trying to do – I was trying to please everyone else apart from myself, and therefore not making these interactions high quality when they occurred.

So, I'd encourage you to look at the following, which hopefully you will now have done:

Step	Things to do	Reflection and further builds
Step 1	Where do you see your priorities in terms of balancing your energy sources?	Do you see any points of focus you can't support?
Step 2	Really reflect on your friendships and how much they are bringing you positive energy and supporting your goals.	Try (as much as possible) to ensure you are spending time only with those who inspire you and give you momentum.
Step 3	Prioritise family time – especially with those you like!	Try to ensure that the balance of time is high with those family members who give you positive energy, wherever possible.

Step	Things to do	Reflection and further builds
Step 4	Exercise is key – schedule to do three to five sessions a week.	Actually DO three to five sessions of exercise of some type each week!
Step 5	Plan and execute your sleep.	Rather than leaving it to chance!
Step 6	Me time!	Have some!

How I personally broke through this

I am lucky to have refined a lot of my personal friendships in my life to those who are always supportive of major changes, but this has only come through a journey of being super-aware of how people affect me. My major recommendation here is to schedule family time (or close friends if you don't have immediate family) and then turn the phone off while you are with them. I can't tell you the difference it makes, so please do try it. You'll also find it so much easier to focus on achieving your 'target self' personal vision.

If you feel these areas are already good, then book some time with someone to unlock something you've been putting off for yourself – a physiotherapist, an osteopath, a massage therapist, a visit to the doctor – just do it today.

If you want more

If this chapter has piqued your interest, you can find more resources, including videos and workbooks, at www.drgeraintevans.com

chapter 6

'T' – Targets for this year

How others have broken through this

'Limitations live only in our minds. But if we use our imaginations, our possibilities become limitless.'

Jamie Paolinetti

Time to put some markers down for the next year. Why just the next year? For me, it is key to focus on a short period of time when we can actively control what happens. We need to use the 'target self' of the future to govern our choices now, but let's focus on progress you can really achieve – not things so lofty that you will fail immediately.

This chapter will utilise my own 'SIMPLE' framework to ensure that you can set effective objectives that are well constructed, measurable and, uniquely, have a return on investment. So, for now, let's go back to the 'think big' picture, but with a laser-like focus on goals you want to achieve in this coming year.

- -

You might be thinking. . .

You say: 'I know I need to change, I can see the future – but I don't know how to begin to get there.'

I say: 'Focus your energy on completing an initial period of progress towards your future; it might start to feel more achievable!'

- -

SIMPLE stands for Scope, Impact, Money, Progress, Learn, End – simple, right? Let's get into it.

Do one thing NOW

Don't overthink this. Write down (or say, or scream!) some of these thoughts. Some people like to do this as a more detailed version of the 'future' timeline we looked at in Chapter 2 (when we addressed the past).

Work over the timeframe that makes sense to you of course, but I'd suggest for now working a year ahead when implementing my SIMPLE framework. This world is a crazy turbulent place at the best of times, and the pace of change is exponential. You've probably already found that sometimes 'life just gets in the way' and you also can't predict massive life events, so I don't want us to get into too much of a long-term mapping exercise. But I do want to stretch your thinking on what this point in the future – your vision – can look like by setting longer term aspirations on where you want to be, so we can once again begin to set up what the details of the next steps are for next year, as you progress towards the end of this one's objectives.

Do one thing NOW

Fast forward into the future a little – what will you be celebrating achieving? Some of you may have a whole host of items to aim for already, some of you may have never even thought about it! Both are okay – we are going to use this chapter to add some structure and, hopefully, therefore make things a lot more achievable.

Create your new end-of-year status

Where, who and what do you want to be in a year from now? To get to the place you visualised, we are going to work through a process to develop a simple 'end-of-year status' for you that we can use to form some objectives to work through for most of this year.

How others have broken through this

'If you are working on something exciting that you really care about, you don't have to be pushed. The vision pulls you.'

Steve Jobs

Before we continue, here are a few health warnings that might differentiate my own personal approach from others you may be aware of, or have heard of. I really want you to embrace the theme of being ambitious, but I also want you to focus on being kind to yourself, as well as others – both of which are mandatory to ongoing motivation for most ordinary people, in my view.

Let's start thinking about achieving progress in the next year of your life. Think of it as a multi-layered programme of work that will move you forward in the areas you feel are most important.

Do one thing NOW

In many business methodologies, initiatives that are undertaken by a company are usually to meet a strategic need, and work is then undertaken in a managed 'programme' to enable and help organise the realisation of 'benefits'. In business, this will involve a combination of projects, workstreams and activities in order to deliver the change and outcomes required to enable the benefits. You are no different to a company. Achieving your aims in the coming year is no different. You are going to have to combine a lot of different types of activity to make a real progression.

So, start to think of where you want to be in a year's time – what the activities are that you plan to do. Remember the notes you took on your 'target self' exercise for the future? Let's begin there. Expand on this now by writing up a summary of what has changed for you in ONLY a year's time (no further into the future). Try to add in factual items (we will go into more detail on these shortly), but also give it feeling – if you want to be proud of something, be proud!

Do one thing NOW

Here's an example of a summary you might write of what you've achieved in the space of a year (and, as always, don't self-censor):

'By the end of 2021, things have really changed. I was not happy with how much debt I was in and was not confident about my future career prospects. But by the end of 12 months a lot has changed for me – and for the better. I'm proud to have stabilised my finances, and have reduced my overall debt by 50%. I have begun a programme of learning this year that has seen me read over 20 books and start a new marketing course to get qualified in this discipline. I have also worked hard to get promoted at work, undertaking a project with extra responsibility to demonstrate my commitment and to use my learning. I have been to the gym nearly every day for six months. I am excited and hopeful about what 2022 has in store for me.'

What you are doing here is working out a first step to becoming the 'future you', but I'm suggesting that you need a laser-like focus on only what is immediately ahead of you. Let's aim to do the things that are required to get to the end-state for this year. It's unlikely you can 'jump' immediately to everything you want, so let's do it through a number of smaller steps and work out the best tasks you can to help achieve what you want. The objectives to make the changes you want need always to be consistent with your 'target self' personal vision – only the things you need to do to deliver it should get your total focus now. Yes, life is always going to 'be there', and you'll handle it – this is about moves (big and small) that are going to create a new version of you and your life.

Detailing objectives (SIMPLE formula)

I hope this is useful to 'bring alive' how to put together objectives. But first, let's reflect on if they are good enough. There are many methodologies you can use to do this. One of the most popular ones is called 'SMART'. The 'SMART' framework was designed to ensure that any objectives are well constructed and measurable. SMART stands for Specific, Measurable, Actionable, Realistic and Timebound. The themes of SMART are super useful to see if they wake up some thoughts in your mind – my main thought when I started doing this was, wow, I've literally never considered objectives like these in my personal life!

I really like the principles of SMART, but I also feel that it lacks some element of iteration and 'chunking up' of tasks, and also some realism about financials – in my experience the main reason things do not get completed.

So, here is my alternative SIMPLE formula for writing down and structuring your end-of-year state vision objectives – see what you think!

'S' for scope (what do you want to achieve?)

What do you want to achieve? Now, ask yourself again – what do you really want to achieve, what exactly is it and by when do you want to achieve it? As it 'says on the tin' – describing the 'scope' of what you want to do in a given area needs to be as specific as possible in terms of what you want to achieve and what it looks like when you've done it. Don't worry too much for now about 'how' you are going to do it – the 'P' of progress will be your place to break that down.

The objectives for achieving your vision of your 'target self' and your targets for the year ahead can be big or small – whatever makes sense to you – as long as, in total, they add up to a significant change in how things are presently. The journey to this first major milestone will give you confidence, but keep the objectives realistic – you can't rely on a one-in-a-million shot to come true. This is also part of the reason I believe that key to achieving long-term progress is starting with 'this year' – let's get some serious things done to underpin what might be the future vision of yourself. The main thing is to ask yourself, 'where do I want to be when I do this again in a year's time?'.

For each objective achievability is key. Keep your objectives simple, but progressive. You don't need to suddenly be perfect in the coming year – you just need to do enough to make a change and achieve your 'target self' personal vision.

'I' for impact (how will achieving this objective change your life for the better?)

Write down the things that will have changed, the benefits you feel you are going to release, the positive changes that you will have seen and how you will know you have got there. For an objective to be measurable it needs to be both specific and have an 'outcome' – something that signals it is complete and 'done'. For me, it's key to connect a feeling to this – quantify it for sure, but add how it affects you. An objective to be 'debt free', for example, might read: 'Being debt free means I can save the money I was using for my future now. This makes me more confident about my retirement.'

Describe your objectives in such a way that they are additive, positive and creating value. This can mean adding value to your life and to others' (something that I strongly advocate getting going on as early as possible). Even those suggestions that contain not-so-nice stuff such as 'stop spending' (never easy to do) are designed to create a positive outcome – a shift in how you're seeing things and how you're taking steps towards delivering your dreams.

'M' for money (how are you going to afford to do it?)

Money is considered to be a dirty word or concept by many people, or on the flip side the key to everything. For me, it's a necessary tool – not a necessary evil, I should add. In the right hands it can help you do whatever you need to do. Not all of your objectives will require a component of money, but in my experience many do. Deciding to get qualified in a key discipline because you know it will help you achieve your next career goal is a good example. You will need money to do this, and this means budgeting and planning to pay for it as part of your objective setting. By not hiding this, and not pretending this is a reality, this type of specificity should hopefully enable you to begin to focus on what you will need to do. It also should help you balance-out your objectives – for example, if your main objective is to 'get out of debt', then committing to spending on a training course might hinder this. You *can* do both, but you just need to be realistic about *how* you do it.

'P' for progress (what things are you going to do to know you are closer to completing your objectives?)

Measuring your progress is key to feeling like you are getting some-where. What tasks can you do in each sprint of activity to track progress? Break down each objective into a set of practical moves and actions – this will enable you to take small steps, and will help reduce the pressure of instantly achieving a big area of objectives. Again, don't worry about the 'size' of these steps for now – just try to break down things that seem big into smaller, more digestible chunks. If you are writing a book, for instance, try committing to writing 500 words a day for a year – you'll soon have plenty to edit into your masterpiece.

'L' for learn (what do you need to know in order to achieve this?)

We'll talk a lot about the need to learn in later chapters, and I really encourage you to embrace the idea of needing to learn when you set any new objectives you wish to deliver that are aligned to your 'target self' personal vision. Even if you are an expert in something, there is always more you can do to hone your skills. If you know nothing about something, but feel it's key to growing towards your 'target self' personal vision (for example, getting some coaching on debt management, saving or how to structure your finances), then immediately try to identify the areas you need to improve on in order to achieve your objective. This can also include learning to be more relaxed, more open, more connected – as these traits, too, require a great deal of study, learning and practice to master. Just for the record, if any part of you is afraid to ask for help, make this an objective in itself.

'E' for end (when will this be done by?)

Even if you follow my advice here to the letter, it is not easy. However, the more we think in terms of properly quantified and specific structured goals, the better. Think about what it will look like when it's done, how you will break it up and achieve it, step by step, and of when you are focused on having it completed by.

Key here is to consider whether your objectives are achievable in the time you have set yourself. Are they controllable, actionable? For example, it is preferable to set an objective of 'begin a marketing course' rather than 'complete a marketing course', as it may not be possible to do that in the allotted time period. Really try to only put down things you can do in the time you have!

Here is an example of what this structure might look like for you:

	S	I	M	P	L	E
	Scope	Impact	Money	Progress	Learn	End
Objective number	What exactly is the objective and what will it look like when you've achieved it?	How will this improve your life for the better?	Great idea, but how much will this cost?	What tasks can you perform in each sprint of activity in order to track progress?	What further skills do you need to complete this?	When will you know it is achieved, and by when?
1						
2						
3						
4						
5						

Okay, so you have your 'target self' personal vision, now let's begin to break this down into a bit more granular detail. For example, using the sample statement shown previously, you might choose to write:

1 **I'm proud to have stabilised my finances, and have reduced my overall debt by 50%.**
By the end of this year/month/week, I will have reduced my credit card balance from £10,000 to £5,000. To achieve this, I will:

- shred the credit card;
- set up a direct debit for £400 per month.

2 **I have begun a programme of learning this year that has seen me read over 20 books.**
By the end of 20XX, to achieve this I will:

- create a budget of £20 per month to buy books (£10 each);
- drink one fewer coffees each day to free up £20 per month;
- research a number of books in my area of interest (marketing) and start by buying three titles recommended to me by my mentor;
- stop taking my phone to bed;
- ensure I get to bed an hour before my usual bedtime.

3 **I will start a new course to get qualified in my discipline.**

- I need to budget for the course. I will afford this through taking out an APR payment plan to make it more affordable;
- I need to investigate options near my work/home;
- I need to consider the best day/time slot to make things sustainable;
- I need to begin the course as soon as possible this year – and at the latest by September.

4 **I have also worked hard to get promoted at work.**
To achieve this, I will:

- schedule a meeting with my line manager/HR support to discuss my ambitions;

- research a number of additional responsibilities I might be able to take on in my company, before I go into the interview;
- ensure actions from the meeting are documented and agreed;
- agree a follow-up each quarter to mark progress.

5 **I will undertake a project with extra responsibility to demonstrate my commitment and to use my learning.**
Through my learning I will:

- identify a key single growth area for me to build my skills and knowledge in;
- watch 10 YouTube videos on the topic;
- discuss this with my mentor monthly, as a minimum, to advance in the topic.

6 **I have been to the gym nearly every day for six months.**

- I will try a number of gyms, both local to where I live and also close to my work, to ascertain the best fit for me;
- I will commit to going to the gym a minimum of four times a week.

7 **I have developed some exciting new friendships.**

- I have pushed myself to attend some networking events to meet new people;
- I have spent more time with acquaintances I liked, but had not focused on previously;
- I have identified friends who do not bring positivity to me, and reduced or removed them from my life.

8 **I am excited and hopeful about what 2021 has in store for me.**
I am clear on what 2021 needs to look like and have documented my new objectives.

Let's see how one of these might look in terms of my proposed SIMPLE framework:

Objective number	S Scope	I Impact	M Money	P Progress	L Learn	E End
	What exactly is the objective and what will it look like when you've achieved it?	How will this improve your life for the better?	Great idea, but how much will this cost?	What tasks can you perform in each sprint of activity in order to track progress?	What further skills do you need to complete this?	When will you know it is achieved, and by when?
1	I'm proud to have stabilised my finances and am now paying off my personal debt much faster	I have reduced my overall debt by 50% (below £5,000 from £10,000)	£5,000	• shred the credit card • set up a direct debit for £400 per month	Better Excel skills (i.e. being able to calculate formulas)	My debt is below £5,000
2						
3						
4						
5						

75

Your 'target self' personal vision is not the place to worry too much about 'threats' to your achievements – we'll develop some other tools for helping on this as we progress through the text. In later chapters we are going to consider working with a range of stakeholders on what might be a challenging journey, involving changes to things such as attitudes, behaviours and working practices. We'll also address whether to update your goals as you go along.

After much procrastination (so don't feel bad if that is your instinct too – although please do fight it!), I really did all of the things I'm suggesting in this chapter, and I really found them all incredibly hard. The main thing I realised was that I spent so much time worrying about what other people need, I never put any focus on giving time to figure out what I needed. I was always thinking, planning, coming up with new ideas, new schemes, doing new things, but I never paused and reflected on 'why' and 'where' I was going, and I rarely thought about what I could do in a year. Once I did, I made massive progress – and you will too.

Steps to execute your plan every day

I am very aware that a lot of the suggestions in this text are forcing you (gently I hope!) to continually come up with new objectives and areas to focus on. I know this is hard if you've never done this before – never considered where you want to put your energies, let alone prioritise them! Review the steps below with a firm 'less is more' attitude. Make sure you are comfortable you can achieve things, but equally make sure they are stretching you to move things forward in the way you now want.

Step	Things to do	Reflection and further builds
Step 1	Find some space to consider what you want to have achieved by this time next year.	Write an 'end-of-year' vision for what you'd like to say about yourself in a year's time.

Step	Things to do	Reflection and further builds
Step 2	Create a list of four to eight specific things you want to have 'done' by the end of the next year.	Try to be as specific as you can in terms of what you want to do.
Step 3	Review your list and ensure your objectives meet all parts of the 'SIMPLE' formula.	Are you really quantifying what you want to do – is it specific enough? Are you sure you know the criteria for when it is done?
Step 4	Consider if you have too many objectives.	If you have written down a lot of objectives, do a review of them to ensure that they are realistic. I love the enthusiasm, I really do, but for now, consider delivering a smaller set, and if you really exceed yourself then go for more next time!
Step 5	What are your priorities?	It is great that you've got so many goals, but make sure you have a sense of priority – remember, things in life do happen and things get in the way. Try to do all of them, but know the ones that matter the most.

How I personally broke through this

You need a list of things you want to do. You may not want to go into the granular detail I have, but you do need a list. It needs to exist. Honestly, I did my first one for 2018 while enjoying a nice drink on the 26th December 2017 at my lovely parents-in-law's house. It was just a simple list of things I was going to aim to achieve in 2018.

> So, using your future vision of yourself, now ask yourself:
> 'where do I want to be in a year from now?'.
>   Make a list, and you'll have a constant reminder of what
> the priority is – a positive focus and outcome. Try to enjoy
> the challenge – don't fear it, but push it and see what you can
> make happen.

If you want more

If this chapter has piqued your interest, you can find more resources, including videos and workbooks, at www.drgeraintevans.com

chapter 7

'S' – Sidetrackers

This chapter focuses on removing, or reducing, what I call 'sidetrackers' – everything from distractions that are blocking your progress on something through to sources of real daily pain. We'll explore some simple remedies for tackling and, where possible, removing these, so they don't get in the way of you achieving your targets.

Connected to this, we'll also address the lack of preparedness in our daily life that is a big creator of stress for most of us. We'll try to use some practical examples from daily life, and I'll suggest some new tools and techniques to remove key moments of stress to enable you to focus on a growing sense of achievement.

Get to know your blockers

I appreciate that it might seem a little counter-intuitive to launch into a deep discussion on blocks, problems and hurdles, now that you are super-energised by creating your goals for this year and your 'target self' personal vision. This is not designed to remove momentum, I just believe we need to tackle what might stop you head on – to really own what might derail you so that you know it, expect it and have a strategy to deal with it. Otherwise, guess what, you'll begin something but get knocked off course – you may even give up, and we are not looking to give up on your 'target self'. The good news is that, by handling what are known as 'blockers', you'll be making better progress, as problems and issues are dealt with progressively. Let's get going!

I'd really encourage you to develop a heightened awareness of 'blockers', as these are everywhere – financial, emotional, personal. Identifying those things that block you (that create a sensation of being 'stuck' in your mind), and reviewing and reflecting on how they have affected you at any point, is key to developing strategies to tackle them every time they occur.

Pause for a second and think through things that frequently get stuck in your mind, or you get stuck on – I call these 'splinters' in my conscious. Was it hard to come up with anything? Let's go through some types of splinters that might be blocking you. Splinters are found in your mind, your soul, your karma – you name it. You know what I'm talking about – a person, a situation, a memory, a desire that's just, well, 'stuck' in your mind. I actually found writing all of mine down into a list helped to get them out of my mind and in a form I could control.

Emotional blockers

'Emotional blockers' are thoughts and feeling you have deep down inside you that trigger certain emotional reactions to things. Do you get a feeling that stops you doing things normally? Do you fear the outcome in some way? Does it feel like there is a wall stopping you (blocking you)? Do you procrastinate?

Do one thing NOW

Write down some of the times you've felt strong emotional feelings about something. Is there anything that seems to be common among them? What do you think this might mean for you?

Financial blockers

Wow, this is a tough one! I am not a genius in observing that a lot of life and its blockers are based on our financial circumstances. How often is money the reason you do – or don't do – something? Does the fear of not having enough money cause you to give up and spend it anyway? Does the fear of losing what you have block you from doing anything proactive with it?

> # Do one thing NOW
>
> Write down the times you feel that 'money' has been a factor in blocking you doing something. What did it feel like? How could you have changed things?

People blockers

I don't know about you, but I get blocked by some people. Perhaps they are people you feel have done you wrong in some way, or someone you just don't click with? Or perhaps it is someone who intimidates you? Think of them as the 'opposite' feeling to what you get when you feel supported and loved by someone. Again, note these people down, and see what patterns emerge.

> # Do one thing NOW
>
> Remember, you don't need to compare yourself to anyone, or worry about what others are doing. As Marie Forleo said, 'Comparison is creative kryptonite. Stay in your own game.'

Now you've got a list of your blockers, begin to think of them as beliefs that are forming barriers to your positive, forward progress. However, by completing this exercise, you now 'own' them a lot more. You can look at them on a piece of paper and they hopefully seem a little less intimidating.

Let's now focus on some quick wins in these situations – some strategies to change your view of these blockers.

Strategies to remove blockers

I've come to think, while on my break, that procrastination is the single most dangerous thing in terms of achieving what you want in life. I think it's particularly pernicious, as it is not that you don't have any idea or concept of what you want to do. You DO, and you normally have a lot of ideas, but you can't get them going.

A technique that I have used in this area is developed by Mel Robbins, known as the 'Five Second Rule'. A lot of people I speak to have not heard of this, so it is worth going over here in a bit of detail, as it's super useful. It works well with the small steps and incremental planning that I really believe is key, and it will help give you the push you might need in the key moments when you don't feel like doing something (but know you should!).

Mel's theory is that if you feel like you are hesitating, holding back or stopping from doing something, you need to take physical action WITHIN FIVE SECONDS, or your brain will 'kill the instinct' to do the thing you want to do in an act of protection. Mel sees the counting down from five, four, three, two to one as crucial, and when you hit one, the next thing to do is 'go' and take action. She gives some great examples of when this is useful, such as speaking up during a meeting, exercising or not grabbing that doughnut.

Mel came up with the idea, knew it worked and then did some research to confirm that there is a scientific basis as a form of metacognition, or a way to trick your brain to make sure it helps you achieve your greater goals – rather than trying to protect you against them by 'keeping you safe' and away from anything scary, uncertain or hard.

Mel found out that this is due to the prefrontal cortex (which you might well have read about in other motivation books). This part of the brain gets very involved in planning, decision making and working towards achieving goals – but it does not necessarily want to help you do that. By counting down from five, you then take deliberate action and push yourself out of autopilot – basically turn on your prefrontal cortex to get it to help you!

Attached to this, Mel also talks about the principle of momentum, where the initial amount of energy needed to start a reaction ('activation energy') is much higher than the amount of energy you then need to keep it going. This links to the 'Progress Principle', which Harvard Business School has demonstrated is the key to happiness and productivity.

- -

You might be thinking. . .

You say: 'I don't have time to stop and think. I'm too busy.'

I say: 'Give yourself permission to become *yourself* as soon as possible.'

- -

I'm assuming that, if you are reading a chapter a week of this text, you are hopefully now a few weeks into trying to establish better patterns and delivering on your 'target self' personal vision. Tough? Not started yet? If the former, read on – if the latter, stop reading and at least try the 'Do one thing' actions from each of the chapters and restart here!

So, assuming it's the former – wow! Let's stop for a bit – how are you? Well done for getting this far into a text like this and making positive changes in your life.

We'll talk about accelerating this with some iterative thinking and short sprints of focused activity in Chapter 10, where not everything is going to go perfectly. It's time to consider how all of this change is affecting you, and if you need some course correction to ensure this really is the best year of achievement for you so far.

You are now dealing with making difficult changes in your life. You have had some ups and downs, and I hope averaging as just 'being okay'. What has been a struggle? Where did you first wobble, and where did you fall off the proverbial wagon pretty much immediately?

First of all, zero judgement from me – elements of what you are doing are going to be very tough, and I'm sure already have been. They were for me too – you are not alone. We need to focus on being a little kinder to ourselves, and maybe understand what 'story' we may still be telling ourselves in order to remember and re-grasp the reasons we decided to make such positive changes from our initial personal reflection in Chapter 1. Before we hit the accelerator pedal, let's just pause a little, reflect, and then hopefully you'll feel like reading on to Chapter 10 with some refreshed impetus to progressing forward into the months ahead and smashing your 'target self' personal vision goal.

Create a 'what's wrong?' list

Sometimes things that are sidetracking us are not as dramatic as major life blockers. Sometimes things just don't feel quite right, do they?

I've found that, again, through recording and reflecting on things, often it's just simple recurring experiences – or outcomes from some more 'fun' experiences – that are the cause of so much sidetracking. In the moment, it feels deep and very difficult to handle feelings.

So, another simple tactic I've developed is creating a 'what's wrong?' list (I'm going to stop apologising for more and more lists now – you need lists, okay!) of things I can check in with if I feel a bit down, demotivated or misaligned.

Most of mine are pretty simple. For example, they might include:

- Have I been drinking alcohol too much?
- Have I not been to the gym in two days?
- Have I not got my eight hours of sleep for more than two days straight?
- Am I not talking about something that is bothering me, which I could address or share with someone else?
- Am I anxious about a task I have not done and is it causing me to not take action?

The key to this list is to recognise what you need to take action on. It's a pretty simple mechanism – just go through the list and once you hit the thing(s) you've not done, you might well be getting your answer. At the very least, addressing the 'one thing' you've not done might change your mindset and state – and, you never know, it might be just what was bothering you most.

Create a 'known distraction' list

This is a brilliant and fun one to tackle, as you get to have a bit of a laugh at yourself! We all get distracted. You've probably got distracted reading this. You've probably checked your phone (don't do that in bed, obviously), had a snack or fallen asleep. If you are on your iPad or laptop, you might have quickly checked a couple of highly urgent emails. If you are on a plane or train you might have paused to consider which new movie you want to watch, pretending you are not going to watch *Pacific Rim. . .* again.

So, for the next day, notice when your attention begins to. . . begins to wander. Note down what distracts you. What stopped you from doing the very thing you were doing. Particularly pay attention to when you are doing your hour, or equivalent, of work in the morning. For example:

- Did your phone go ping, and you picked it up? Was that notification more important than focusing on your 'target self' personal vision for this year? Maybe consider turning off the audio notifications, or even (shock horror!) the phone itself.

- Did you suddenly break away from the highly prioritised task you were working on to check an email, or do that other 'thing' quickly? Why not quickly note down that task, and go back to it once you've completed the priority task(s) you set yourself to do that day? It was not crucial last night, so is it now?

- Did you decide you urgently need that extra coffee, right now? Bring in a flask of coffee to your desk tomorrow.

Later (in Chapter 9), we are going to talk a lot more about saying 'no' in the wider context of your life and goals, so you need to build some muscle now by at least recognising the 'bad' behaviour that is distracting you from achieving your daily, fortnightly and yearly goals.

So, you get the picture – don't character assassinate yourself, but just note the distractions down, have a bit of a laugh at yourself and try to not let them affect you in future!

No	Things that typically distract me	Actions I should take if this known distraction happens
1		Check my distraction list!
2		
3		
4		
5		
6		
7		
8		
9		
10		

Create your 'splinter' list

As I began to implement the various ways of working that I am detailing in this text, I noticed that I had various 'things' emerging in my daily rituals of getting prepared and getting out of the door vaguely on time. Different from the blockers I've detailed previously – these were funny things, thoughts, ideas, little things that kept coming up. Sometimes they were not so specific but more general, and usually not single-task items. Sometimes they were just the more mundane or nebulous parts of life – things that I was just, well, 'not feeling good about'.

For example, these could be things like 'I need to save more in my pension', or 'I need to think about replacing the car soon'. These are things that will become actions and to-dos for you to complete, but they aren't defined or a priority right now. Some of these things might be tougher to take. Difficult experiences or events that just keep coming back to you. Often it feels like they are just stuck – this is why I call them 'splinters'. They don't have to be painful ones – in fact often they are just things we know we need to pay attention to.

I'd often find these little things kept on popping into my mind. So, one day, I created a separate list (yes, sorry, another list – they are important!) in my to-do list app called 'splinter list', and began to document these thoughts and feelings. I found that my mind quietened down – almost as though it was relieved to have these things off its back and somewhere else.

This list has since become a really important asset for me in my overall organisation. I scan through it every week or so to ensure that none of the worries is of top importance. My essential to-do list is focused on the positive things I need to do to move my life towards my 'target self' personal vision objectives. We all have things that are bothering us – little worries, thoughts or tasks that we know we need to do at some point soon, but don't need to do now. So, get these out of your mind and somewhere else, so you can focus on the positive development towards your yearly goals.

Creating a splinter list will help you 'own' them a little more – if you can see them all on a list, I feel it is easier to deal with them as they occur. This is how I structure this:

1 What 'splinters' am I always thinking about?

2 Why might this thought be occurring so often?

3 What am I going to do the next time I think of one of them?

What 'splinters' am I always thinking about?	Why might this thought be occurring so often?	What am I going to do the next time I think of one of them?

What 'splinters' am I always thinking about?	Why might this thought be occurring so often?	What am I going to do the next time I think of one of them?

Now have a go at writing down your own 'splinter' list.

Get to know your stories

> ## How others have broken through this
>
> 'There are no limits to what you can accomplish, except the limits you place on your own thinking.'
>
> Brian Tracy

In the previous chapters we've looked at the need to clearly establish who you want to be – and then try to be consistent in your actions in achieving this. However, this is easier said than done and we might feel there are deeper things blocking our progress. Another way to look at this is what 'consistency rules' do you have for who and how you want to be? We've also recognised the feeling of someone having something over you, and how to laugh in the face of it. However, sometimes we also need to recognise that it goes deeper than that.

One thing we need to realise is that we often might be telling ourselves a story – and a fictional story at that. Many authors in the motivation space are big on the idea of changing your story, as it informs everything about how you frame things. The story can result in you characterising yourself as 'an anxious person', or 'I'll never succeed', or 'I'm not good enough'. It can go so deep and be so subconscious that you may not even be aware of it. To become aware of it, watch how you frame things verbally – perhaps using negative phrases such as 'let's kill a bit of time before. . . '.

The principles of narrative therapy are useful to work through this. Narrative therapy is a type of counselling that essentially views people as being separate from their problems, thereby allowing them to get some distance from the issue or story. This way, you can look at something objectively, and see if it is actually helping you, protecting you in some way or in fact hurting you. Try this: deeply reflect inwards and get a sense of what you believe about yourself at the deepest part of your core. As with so many things we've covered, this is only about perspective – you can change that perspective or even totally re-write your story. If you are already undertaking tasks that get you closer to your 'target self' personal vision, then consider using these achievements as 'evidence' to yourself (to your inner-story) that you are making changes to your thought patterns and behaviours – that you are capable of so much more. As you begin to implement positive and productive new ways to approach your life, your future is changing – and the potential to stop identifying yourself by your problems is so much closer than you think.

Your life story will continue to evolve, but you don't need to live in the past. You can write whatever future you want for yourself – you just need to begin to 'become' that person through taking action. Good news if you are already doing that. If you've read this far and are not yet implementing something, consider going back and trying some of the steps.

From a personal perspective, and linked to the principle of not giving myself credit, over time I began to reframe my story to crack the terrible habit (which I'm sure many of you may share) and take pride in what I have achieved, instead of automatically thinking people don't want to hear about us doing well. The old saying 'pride cometh before a fall' is still incredibly pervasive in society.

Working on this aspect of yourself takes some effort, for sure, but even entering into a dialogue with yourself can help to break old cycles and change your future. You don't need to continue to live the 'old story' any more. Be proud of yourself – give yourself a little credit.

I also know how hard this is. What I used to lovingly call my 'working-class chip on shoulder' would kick in at every single juncture that I achieved anything. It would tell me that of course I should be achieving these things – I'd been weak and underachieving for so long.

If someone paid me a compliment I would just 'white noise' it out. Not take it in but simply focus on whatever negative aspects of the conversation I could.

Funny thing is, when I began to realise I was doing okay in terms of achieving my aims, I had a breakthrough. I learned to actually begin to give myself credit for doing well by literally saying one line to myself – even if in my heart I did not mean it: 'You did well there'. I would give myself a literal or virtual pat on the same shoulder my chips used to be. More on that shortly.

The thing I now want you to try here is something similar that feels connectable, doable, but is not going to push you too far out of your comfort zone. When you get a minute, try actually practising saying your one line where you acknowledge you've done well to yourself – get used to it basically!

Incidentally, if some of you are reading this and thinking 'this is crazy, I'm totally comfortable giving myself credit', then great! Credit to you. Still try what I'm suggesting though – it will make you feel even better!

Steps to execute your plan every day

The work I'm recommending in this chapter is hard – it is hard to build momentum. However, by introducing a simple morning routine designed to support learning it is really amazing the progress you can make. Doing a daily 'stand up' also allows you to pause before you engage, and reflect on 'why' and 'where' you are going.

Step	Things to do	Reflection and further builds
Step 1	Write down some of the times you've felt strong feelings about emotions, finances or people 'stopping you' doing something.	Is there anything that seems to be common among them? What do you think this might mean for you?
Step 2	Try the Five Second Rule!	Next time you feel you are hesitating or procrastinating, try taking a deep breath and counting backwards from five to one – see if it works for you!
Step 3	Reflect on practical day-to-day blockers – what stopped you doing what you needed to do yesterday? Capture a list to spot any patterns.	Reflect also on what's gone well – what can you repeat again? Then reflect on what's not gone so well – what might derail you in the future if you don't address it? Where might you need support?
Step 4	Create your list of known 'splinters' – things that block you – so you 'own' them, not them owning you.	Consider your own personal story and what you might be telling yourself – don't forget to give yourself permission to be that future version of yourself, and if you can't, note down what is stopping you (for now!).
Step 5	Review the progress you've made so far in achieving your 'target self' personal vision and ensure it's still what you want.	Actively give yourself some 'credit' for achievements through the use of a new key phrase or action.

How I personally broke through this

The game-changer for me in all of this was actually taking a minute to reflect on why I was feeling the way I was in any given moment. I had a variety of blockers and recurring thoughts that often really heightened my stress levels. Capturing and managing these freed up a lot of spare processing capacity in my brain as I didn't need to think about them so much – I could just recognise them, be okay with them, and move on.

If you want more

If this chapter has piqued your interest, you can find more resources, including videos and workbooks, at www.drgeraintevans.com

chapter 8

—

'E' – Everyday routines

This chapter focuses on how to reflectively implement (yes, really implement rather than just reading about!) some of the traditional suggestions made by motivation books, such as 'morning' and 'evening' lists, and tackles difficult, but undeniably powerful, things such as journalling – reflecting proactively on elements you've included in your target self.

How others have broken through this

'Perspective and perseverance are prime in all things.'

Samoa Joe

You might be thinking. . .

You say: 'Right. I need a plan.'

I say: 'Focus more on being prepared, not just organised.'

You will by now have thoroughly thought through your 'target self' – and have a meaningful list of targets for this year. You are starting to think really carefully about how you want to grow, and what this personal growth looks like for you. You know change is going to mean removing blockers in your life (whether they be emotional, financial or people) and implementing simple project management of tasks.

You've already begun to listen to your heart, thereby (hopefully!) gaining a better understanding of yourself through reflection. And you've begun to tackle your new focus with energy and commitment.

This chapter could logically have been called 'Planning' as it will help you work out a detailed plan to deliver your 'target self' personal vision. We will discuss how to iterate, chunk things up and do an unprecedented amount of work in a short period of focused, two-week bursts, but before we get into that I want to give you a short cut line of thinking that has absolutely transformed my life: getting prepared, not just organised.

What do I mean by that? Let me explain.

I consider myself an 'organised' person, but I often found myself frustrated. This would often occur when I did not have the ONE thing I needed to have with me – an iPhone battery, or specifically, my laptop charger – this was the thing that took me over the edge, and made me realise something was not working.

I was desperately trying to assemble the bits I needed for a family weekend trip visiting relatives in Wales. It was a familiar scenario: taxi coming to collect us; running out of time; grabbing books, clothes and a few bits for myself. While rapidly trying to get everything together, I paused, looked at my laptop charger and thought 'nah, I don't need it – my laptop is charged', and didn't take it.

I had a bit of work to do that weekend (this was obviously before I realised this line of thinking and action was taking me nowhere) on some data I had to compile a report on for a management meeting, which it had been too late to action on Friday afternoon. I had quantified the time I felt it would take (a few hours at most) and was ready to complete it while the family went out to the local beach – I was all organised. But, in the end, it was late on the Sunday night by the time I got to it, I had to do more work than I expected, my battery failed and I could not complete the work. I had not saved it to the cloud and there was no laptop in the house to rebuild it. This led to me getting up at 4am on the Monday morning (not to meditate!) and having a stressed-out start to the week.

I should have trusted my instinct. A micro-moment of pure, unadulterated indolence at not wanting to bend down, unplug a plug and put it in a bag – possibly a minute of activity, in total. A lot of things are ridiculous about this. Why, in the moment, did I not plan for the possibility of having to do more work, and therefore of the battery failing? Why couldn't I foresee this situation? Why didn't I trust my initial judgement? Why did I not listen to myself? Why, why, why? (Cue picture of me screaming on my knees in the rain somewhere!)

When I began to actively reflect on this in my 'freeform' thinking, and having permitted myself a 'bit of a moan' in my journalling (although, remember, it's not a 'be negative about yourself' journal!), I came to the conclusion that while I was normally a pretty organised person, small things kept on happening to trip up my day. Neither was I preparing for what I needed to do, nor was I predicting relatively simple things that had a strong likelihood of occurring, let alone more 'unexpected' things that might happen to derail me. There were (and still are, as I am still working to get better at this daily!) a lot of reasons for this. Let's look at a few of these to see if they might also resonate with you:

- I was always rushing. Funny, but no matter how much I planned to get up early, set the alarms, limited my snoozes and had positive energy bursting out of me for the day, I always seemed to be rushing. When you rush, your brain is shouting instructions at you, other people are probably also shouting instructions at you, and the 'time to leave' is rapidly approaching.

- I was not checking the status of things that could later derail me.

- I had my overall to-do list clear, I knew what I had to do, but I was not clear on priorities – on what I had to do before leaving the house that morning.

- I was not helping myself to get some quick wins and limit the number of things I needed to think about when the 'rushing' maelstrom hit.

So, from these reasons, I came up with the idea of delineating between being 'organised' and being 'prepared' – and I have found that my life has improved massively in small ways that all add up to more impetus, confidence and readiness for when I get smacked by a curveball. Here are some practical suggestions to work with that I hope will help you too.

How others have broken through this

'You don't have to be great to start, but you have to start to be great.'

Zig Ziglar

Create your 'evening' list

If it's a Sunday, you might be getting that 'back-to-school' nervous feeling. If it's a normal, bog-standard Wednesday, you might be more relaxed, figuring you'll, well, figure it out in the morning.

However, think about the times when 'the night before' is something 'big' – it can be stressful, hard to sleep, and while you might do some things last minute, I am sure many of you reading this have managed a little preparation beforehand, such as packing at night before getting up early for a flight, or making sure you've ironed your shirt for a crucial interview. So, in some circumstances, being 'ready' for things is not a totally unnatural feeling.

My breakthrough on this was to apply this thinking not only to 'special occasions' (if an interview can ever be seen as that!), but also to everyday preparation.

As an early-morning action (when I was not rushing around for once!), I brainstormed all of the things that I felt could help minimise stress and disruption and remove as many potential problems and obstacles as possible before the following day begins.

After a bit of experimentation, I now work to the following list pretty much every evening of my life (but not every evening – as I covered in Chapter 3, implementing daily objectives as part of your 'target self' personal vision is great, but don't be too hard on yourself if you only hit them six times out of seven each week).

I have it printed out next to my bed, on the back of the door so I see it before I lock it and next to the kettle where I make my hot-water bottle (yes, I could write a whole book on those too!).

My list is called 'PREPARED, NOT JUST ORGANISED – BEFORE BED/REFLECT AND PRE-PLAN' and this is what is on it:

1 Have you done a journal entry for your day?

2 Have you taken time to be thankful?

3 Have you prioritised your to-do list for tomorrow[*]?

4 Are you ready for everything you are doing tomorrow, as much as you can be?

5 Have you checked where you are going first tomorrow, and if you have enough time to get to the second place?

6 Have you checked all transport options to get there (including walking, cycling, train, underground, taxi or driving?) and figured out what is optimal?

7 Have you set your alarm to give you time to get ready?

8 Have you set your alarm to give you an extra 15 mins to get ready?

9 Are all of your clothes out ready?

10 Thinking ahead – what could go wrong, in terms of what you can control?

Simple stuff, really, and things that make sense to me. I have most of them memorised now, but I like to go through each of them as a checklist to ensure I am as prepared as possible – sometimes they are more relevant than others, but most are consistent for each day. If I have not done something I need to, I do it before going to bed.

Getting your clothes ready is a killer one for me. Not that I really take much time to get ready, or procrastinate on what I'm wearing too much, but isn't it amazing how many pitfalls there can be in compiling an outfit? Keeping up with the ironing, finding the right shoes, favourite socks being in the wash, or forgetting to go to the dry cleaners to pick up your suit. There is also an ancillary benefit to this preparation – it reduces what is called 'decision fatigue', where we get jaded and drained by constantly making decisions about things, even if they appear relatively small on the surface. Allegedly, certain

* More on that one coming up!

well-known people, such as Barack Obama and Mark Zuckerberg, reduce the options in their everyday clothing to one or two outfits in order to limit the number of decisions they make in a day!

Your action is to come up with your own list of things that you know, hand on heart, will help you be prepared for the next day.

You might be thinking. . .

You say: 'But what if I can't do it?'

I say: 'Time to take the stabilisers off. You are going to wobble, you are going to fall, but you are going to learn to pedal faster – and, ultimately, you are going to be able to ride.'

This chapter will now build on the aspects of learning and reframing our blockers we've already learned in order to develop some core daily practices to help achieve the objectives of our 'target self' personal vision – it's time to unleash yourself. You have the power to do whatever you want (within reason – learning to fly might take a little while longer, but it is possible!). Unleashing the energy is not always about aiming for the impossible. As we've discussed, your goal might be learning to climb Mount Kilimanjaro barefooted or doing 1,000 one-armed press ups, but possibly it's a bit simpler, such as getting out of debt, or getting a better job. Whatever your goal, it is going to require letting go of the things you might have always told yourself.

In early chapters, we focused on ways to accelerate progress and build momentum. In this section I'd like to begin to encourage you to develop your new daily productivity and mindfulness practice on your own terms. It's crucial to find a daily balance between focusing on specific task progression and developing a greater understanding of yourself, and this is going to take us into the somewhat difficult territory of more personal reflection. I found this a particularly difficult thing to begin doing at all, let alone in a structured way, so if you do too, you are definitely not alone.

The good news is there are so many opportunities for 'wins' in this section, I think you'll begin to get a lot out of some of these changes!

Shaping your new 'daily practice'

How others have broken through this

'Build yourself up with one perfectly laid brick each day. Soon you will have a wall. . . '

Tom Bilyeu

Is this your daily practice: roll out of bed having finally given in to the alarm after hitting snooze five times, make the coffee, get in the shower, be late into the office, your phone buzzing with 23 things you have failed to do already? Or maybe it's a chaotic scene of your family getting ready for school, or coming in late after working through the night? The evening is a lot like this too, isn't it? Coming home late, not making it to the gym, grabbing a glass of something on a Tuesday and catching up with Facebook on your phone lying in your bed. If this is your reality, you are not alone, and sometimes that is what you need to do to survive. Zero judgement here, as always.

However, if you're reading this text, I'm guessing you've had a nagging feeling that you'd like to improve somewhat, and if you've made it this far you've now got a new vision for your life and a clearer view on what you want to do by the end of this year. You are also a bit more aware of your potential blockers and things that might trip you up. So, let's get proactive and build up what a day for you is potentially going to look like. Let's start with how some of our super-successful friends do it. A lot of gurus write about how to tackle the beginning and end of the day, so let's dive into that.

Think of these as future 'key achievements' you are aspiring to. It can be anything that feels meaningful to you – for example, reflecting on your past-to-present timeline we looked at in Chapter 2. So, the next action is to write down some more practical ways you feel you could improve your current state of being.

- -

You might be thinking. . .

You say: 'But really, won't people laugh at me and judge me – where do I even start?'

I say (actually. . . my five-year-old really said this, unprompted): 'You can only control your mind, not the weather.'

- -

This chapter will now introduce some key concepts from another project management methodology called Agile (yes, go with me on this as well please!), including crucially providing some structure for achieving daily progress towards the objectives you've just outlined in your wonderful 'target self' personal vision.

Many of you may have heard of 'Agile' (or 'Scrum'), but for those who haven't let's quickly do a bit of a 'beginner's guide'. (Bear with me on the next lot of content as this methodology is just so incredibly useful, and its principles have really transformed my personal and working life – it can be applied to anything and everything. Even better, it has some super-cool terms such as 'planning poker', 'daily stand-ups' and 'sprints' – what's not to like?)

According to the Scrum Alliance and its Agile Manifesto, Agile refers to a set of 'methods and practices based on the values and principles expressed in the Agile Manifesto', which include things such as promoting collaboration, self-organisation and the cross-functionality of teams. Agile was born out of the techniques utilised by innovative Japanese companies such as Toyota, Fuji and Honda in the 1970s and '80s, and in the 1990s Jeff Sutherland created the Scrum framework after finding himself frustrated by projects that were always behind schedule and often over budget. Sutherland and his co-creator, Ken Schwaber, have made the official guide available on scrumguides.org if you want to learn more on this.

Scrum is the framework used to implement Agile development. Scrum is often most used to develop tangible products, and typically begins with a blank whiteboard and a pad of sticky notes (you can do it online with programs such as Trello). It is used to break down complex problems, and then prioritises them into individual tasks – the 'backlog' – or what needs to be done to create the product or, in your case, your 'end-state vision'. In larger teams, these tasks are then delegated to other team members with the skill set best suited to solving each of them.

Scrum also has two really interesting additional 'roles' that will help you in your own journey – the 'Product Owner' and the 'Scrum Master'.

A Scrum starts with the Product Owner, who owns the creation and prioritisation of the backlog, represents the final user's 'best interests' and has the last say in what goes into the final product being produced.

The team undertaking completion of the items on the backlog does so in a concept called a 'sprint' – a predetermined timeframe of usually one-to-two weeks. During the state of 'sprint planning', the team collectively decides what tasks to include in the forthcoming sprint, and who will be responsible for them. A sprint always ends with a review called a 'retrospective', where the team reviews the completed tasks, the work that was done and discusses ways to improve for the next sprint – maybe it's the size of a task that was bigger than expected, or an individual team member who is overloaded. The next sprint is then started, with the team choosing items from the backlog and repeating the process.

During the sprint, the teams also meet every day to give progress updates in a daily Scrum meeting, typically called a 'daily stand-up' because, guess what, they are conducted standing up (good for energy!). They also last no more than 15 minutes (yes, it's true – meetings *can* be only 15 minutes!), and aim to answer three crucial questions:

1 What tasks did you work on/complete yesterday?

2 What tasks will you be working on today?

3 Is there anything blocking your work today that you need help with?

Some simple organisational elements of the stand-up are going to be useful for you to consider implementing yourself: they always occur at the same time, and at a time that works for everyone. In Agile, a team is supported by a person called the 'Scrum Master', who is primarily responsible for helping remove any blockers. Guess what, you are your own personal Scrum Master!

Ask yourself – what did you achieve yesterday?

So, you've got your 'target self' personal vision. Let's begin to break down some tasks. Ideally, stop to do some of these tasks before you read on.

A bit like the focus on one year at a time, I want you to focus on one day at a time in terms of tracking progress. This chapter also begins to deal with beliefs that form blockers to progress, and proposes strategies on how to change them, through developing a better understanding about ourselves, by identifying things that are 'stuck' in our mind, reviewing and reflecting on how they affected that day, and developing key questions to ask ourselves every time they occur.

So, when should you do a review of tasks and plan your next one? A lot of the motivational gurus will say that you should sort out your list of things to do in the evening so you can hit it first thing in the morning. This does work for a lot of people, and they may choose to use this time to journal and reflect on the day. I'd recommend experimenting with this and finding your 'ideal' time to do this organising. We'll come on to the specifics of this in later chapters.

For now, let's get into the habit of reviewing progress. I'm assuming by now you've begun some of your tasks towards achieving your 'target self' personal vision? It might even be the first week of the new year and your commitment to delivering your vision.

So, in basic terms, ask yourself – how did it go yesterday? Did you do more or less than you planned? Reflect on this – what would you do the same or differently tomorrow? Do this as a hands-on activity. Commit to doing it for real – this is a crucial momentum in trying to move forward.

Did you perhaps not do anything towards achieving your aim? Was it a busy day, and you just didn't have time among all of your other commitments? You had to go shopping, drop off the kids, fetch the kids (football was one in our house for a while)? Before you knew it, it was bedtime. Blockers – all blockers. I've been there so, so many times. Let's try to make a breakthrough mentally on this.

What are you going to do today?

How others have broken through this

'Hard work keeps the wrinkles out of the mind and spirit.'

Helena Rubinstein

Okay, let's focus on how to make progress on a daily basis. The key to making progress towards your 'target self' personal vision is to regularly review it to check how much you've done on it. Again, like so much of this text, the focus is on building discipline and rigour by doing things in repeated patterns. Reviewing your priorities for each day is a great place to begin because it allows you to actively think about what you need to achieve, rather than somehow trusting it will happen naturally. Yes, sometimes we do get that unexpected golden hour where we can get into something we've been putting off and really focus on getting it done, but I think we can all recognise these are few and far between in reality.

For now, I'm not looking for you to actually prioritise tasks. Instead I'd like you to begin to recognise patterns in why you did and didn't achieve things you've set out to do. This can go beyond your own 'target self' personal vision. What, in your normal day, do you regularly fail to achieve? Also, think about the inverse of this – when you've really nailed something and you are proud of it, what are the conditions for doing so that facilitated this? I don't want to ponder on this as a bad thing. I believe sometimes the key to achieving things is actually the absence of blockers – things that normally get in your way, that did not this time. Maybe it is how you managed them in that particular situation, or that a unique set of circumstances came together, but almost certainly it was how you managed them that resulted in your achievement of them.

Now, this line of thinking might seem surprisingly negative – managing blockers helped me achieve something? Yes. In fact, everything you are going to do in this coming year to achieve your 'target self' personal vision will be dependent on getting to know your blockers as if they were best friends – keep your enemies closer!

The morning ritual (of the stars)

Many of the most successful self-help and motivation advisors suggest adopting a fixed morning routine to really get motoring first thing. One such advisor is Tim Ferriss – a best-selling author, podcast host and investor in the likes of Uber and PayPal. Tim has talked a lot about this subject and has some interesting practices. For example, the first thing he does each morning is make his bed. This is to ensure that there is one deliberate thing he can control each day, as derived from Naval Admiral William H. McRaven's now famous commencement speech at the University of Texas in Austin in 2014, in which he advocated: 'If you make your bed every morning you will have accomplished the first task of the day. It will give you a small sense of pride, and it will encourage you to do another task and another and another. By the end of the day, that one task completed will have turned into many tasks completed.'

Tim then drinks some tea and has a small breakfast. He spends 20 minutes meditating each morning, followed by a two-minute 'decompression period' where he just lets his mind wander. He indulges in some exercise to wake him up and prime him for the day, and sometimes follows that with a 60-second cold shower (erm, optional, but transformative if you can stomach it!). Okay, so that is a big change from rolling out of bed, checking your phone and putting the kettle/coffee machine on isn't it? But what practical things can we take from this?

Starting with a daily visualisation

One area I'd strongly consider continuing is the visualisation you started when you came up with this year's end-state vison, by doing it on a daily basis in some way. This can take many forms, and timings. One thing I found quite useful was a daily scanning of the 'target self' personal vision and my objectives, just to act as a refresher towards what I am looking to achieve (other, more old-school, advice suggests writing the objectives down fresh every single day).

You might even want to take this to another level by spending some time visualising achieving your goals and objectives in any way that makes sense to you – imagine what it's literally going to be like when you achieve them – what you can see, smell, who you are with – as if you've got some kind of advanced VR headset on! I find this can really help you 'connect' with your vision and begin to believe it can be true – and, guess what, if you are taking steps to achieving it every day then it is coming true.

An extension to this is experimenting with additionally setting an intention for the day – to be a bit better in a specific way, to be forgiving or compassionate on a specific point. I do this one some days, and it does help focus your mind on who you want to be that day.

Another thing I find useful, and have settled on personally, is being a little more macro – focusing on 'themes' I want to stay consistent on every day, not just for one day. This list (sorry, I know, another list, but it's better in an app or on paper than swirling around your head, honestly!) can just summarise a few things you are and are not looking to be, moving forward. This could be things such as 'I want to be a generous person' or 'I'm not going to keep apologising'. They are a lot more abstract than the specifics of your 'target self' vision for your future, of course. These are a little more nebulous, and hard to quantify into 'SIMPLE' objectives, but I find by committing to them as if they were daily 'tasks', it has helped me remind myself of areas to work on.

Making a gratitude list

We do not show gratitude enough, do we? Many motivational and performance coaches believe that showing gratitude every day is the single greatest thing you can do to positively impact your life. For example, Deepak Chopra describes gratitude as an 'immensely powerful force that we can use to expand our happiness, create loving relationships, and even improve our health'. How I do this is by keeping a short list of all the people I want to give thanks for every day:

Who am I grateful for?	Why am I grateful they have entered my life?
1	
2	
3	
4	
5	
6	
7	
8	
9	
10	

Some advisors, such as Bedros Keuilian, also propose that you use this time to actually reach out to the people and tell them specifically what you are grateful for – for example, a quick message outlining how they've impacted your life. I appreciate this might be uncomfortable territory for some of you, so don't feel you have to do this, but, again, it's something to consider for the future. I've started this myself now that I'm a bit further into implementing some of the suggestions in this text and I've been amazed by the feedback, so definitely bear it in mind. First of all, though, remember to be grateful!

Journalling your way – a reflection list

We are probably pretty familiar with the concept of 'journalling'. Since we were kids, we've known about diaries (and may even have kept one at a certain point), and we know that it's good to express and let out our innermost thoughts – so why is this so hard for so many of us? Since taking on some of the actions of this text, I began journalling and kept it up for a while, but I really began to struggle with it. I found it hard to be honest with myself – a bit like I was talking in code to myself.

Eventually, I realised it was the 'non-directed' nature of it that was tripping me up. So now, in my daily practice, I don't just openly journal as Mr Ferriss does, I focus on reflection.

My journal (yes, sorry, another thing to maintain – this will get easier!) is now a series of reflections in a list that matches my 'target self' personal vision. All this is, in practice, is tips, ideas and quotes that come out of my daily learning practice. I just keep it in a list, and often look at it if I feel a bit stuck or just have some time to kill and don't have space to begin a substantive task.

Morning routines for 'normal' people

The routine suggested by the likes of Tim Ferriss is a lot to take on if you are already late for work, have screaming kids wanting breakfast and there's a TV blaring in the background. I have experimented a little with Tim's routine and, honestly, I did find it tough to execute initially, but some of its key elements have proven to be very useful for me. Here are a few tips that I do that might make it work for you too:

1 The first pre-requisite is that your phone is off, or on airplane mode, when you wake (so therefore done before you went to sleep).

I've begun to do this religiously, and while I can't prove it, I feel it is improving my mental state in the morning, as I consciously need to make a change of 'state' to be ready for the deluge of emails, alerts and push messages.

2 For me, my meditation is the first 10 minutes when the alarm goes off. On non-exercise days (see next bit), I will set the alarm one hour earlier than the last time I can wake up – so that I can hit the snooze button, but only once. (Many gurus will say that's already setting my day up for failure, but I don't agree unless you are hitting it three times plus.)

3 Once I am what I call 'officially awake', I don't get out of bed, I sit up a little (to avoid nodding off) and then I spend a few minutes with my eyes closed. First, I try to focus on what I'm grateful for – my family, my life; then I try to focus on what I'm trying to do long term – visualising it; and then, when I feel my mind beginning to wander into specific actions, I open my eyes and get out of bed.

4 I don't always make the bed when I get up, but I do try to do one thing that is an achievement first thing – I'll do a quick bit of tidying up while I am waiting for the kettle to boil or coffee to pour. I try to focus on something annoying – like taking the bins out, or collecting the shoes strewn across the house and putting them into at least a single pile.

5 Then, I'll head to my desk (but any kitchen counter or sofa will do), and do the ONE thing I need to do that's bothering me most (the thing that is 'needling' me).

6 I review my to-do list and, if I have time, I'll do the next-most annoying thing, or I'll begin the morning routine of shower/ second breakfast, getting clothes on, etc.

7 A few mornings a week I'll also get myself out of bed and pretty much immediately do some form of exercise. Key to this, as with everything, is preparation – having your gym clothes next to the bed or door, keys ready, headphones ready. Wake up, and whatever you need to do – five, four, three, two, one – grab any negative thoughts and start shouting those thoughts (quietly if people are sleeping). I'll listen to a motivational speech or

interview. This exercise may come in the form of running, going to a gym, 30 minutes of circuits or body-weight exercises from a class on YouTube, or a bit of aggressive yoga!

How this might look like for you:

Order of events	Morning list
1	
2	
3	
4	
5	
6	
7	
8	
9	
10	

Do one thing NOW

If there is only one thing from my morning to-do list I would suggest, it is to buy a reusable coffee cup and water bottle today, and for everyone in your household, and never leave home without them. I took embarrassingly ages to do this myself.

I was good with the water bottle bit. But it took me an age and, despite best efforts to recycle them, a huge personal contribution to landfill of so many coffee cups before I cottoned on to the reusable cup. Do it today – they are now everywhere – and some of them are such good value that you'll even save money as you save the world. If most of you reading this text do this, the world will be a better place to live in. So please, please do it now if you are out and about, or ASAP if you're online.

Night-time routines for night owls

For those who prefer to be busy at the end of the day, here are some tips for an evening routine:

1 Number one priority is no phone in the bed. NO PHONE IN BED!

2 Try not to eat within 90 minutes of your sleep time.

3 If you have trouble sleeping at night, try not to exercise within two hours of going to bed, and (exercise or not) having a hot bath or shower can really work.

4 Before I retire my phone for the night, I look at my to-do list and think about the three things I need to do to make the next day a success.

5 Read a book – for me, this is a 'real' paper book if I'm at home or an iPad if I'm away somewhere.

6 And just before you go to sleep, how about a spot of meditating.

Order of events	Evening list
1	
2	
3	
4	
5	
6	
7	
8	
9	
10	

Create your 'walk out the door' list

Despite my evening list making a massive difference to my feeling more prepared for what life might throw at me, I quickly realised that I was still having a lot of stressful days due to what I call 'avoidable avoidables' – think of them as some kind of evil cousin to 'controllable controllables'!

My evening list had given me a head start on the day, and taken away a lot of stress, for sure, but, as Don Henley says, a lot can happen 'in a New York minute' (sorry, obscure reference for some of you – I have tried to be cool and contemporary in the rest of the text, but I am old!). My evening list had enabled me to focus on being more organised, but I was still not being super-prepared, and now I realise they are critically different.

So, I built on what I had started and created a morning list too – again with an emphasis on not having to think too hard, having less 'decision fatigue' and avoiding some obvious problems. I brainstormed all of the things that I was usually rushing about doing, things I kept leaving the house with, and documented some of those little details that were tripping me up last minute and throughout the day.

I now have this list on the reverse of our front door – this really helps me focus on the 'morning of', particularly if I'm doing something that day that is quite stressful and requires concentration. And, yes, it really is called the 'AM/GOING OUT OF THE DOOR – DO YOU HAVE WITH YOU?' list:

1 Have you re-checked your route this morning?

2 Have you checked the weather?

3 Do you have a full, refillable bottle of water?

4 Do you have a reusable coffee cup?

5 Do you have a spare plastic bag?

6 Have you put on sun cream?

7 Do you have more sun cream, your sunglasses, hat and umbrella?

8 Do you have your phone, wallet and Oyster card?

9 Have you checked your teeth and hair for 'foreign objects'?

10 Do you have a phone charger cable/plug and a spare phone battery?

11 Is your laptop charged? If not, do you have the cable in your bag?

12 Do you need any adaptors or wires today?

13 Have you got your headphones?

14 Do you need any special or specific item with you today (e.g. a passport)?

It takes less than a minute to check through, and only a minute to sort out if something is missing. But I don't wait until I'm leaving the house to check it, as I also have a copy pinned above the coffee maker and one next to the bathroom mirror!

In the course of a working week, missing some or all of these things has caused me problems. Often not in a major way, but certainly adding to the cumulative stress of an unexpected situation.

Your morning list is all about the mundane little things that you know could come back to haunt you if you don't pay attention. Create your own – or use mine as a starting point.

But, before you go out of the door, you ideally need to have taken a step towards achieving one of your 'target self' personal vision objectives that day. So, let's discuss a simple strategy for that.

Create your prioritised to-do list

We've already talked at length on how to break up your year into achievable objectives, on being optimistic but brutal in terms of focusing on a few key items you can realistically achieve. From that we've produced a 'target self' personal vision that you are now rocking and rolling to.

From there I've encouraged you to document ideas and to-do list items continually – getting them out of your head and into a structured format whenever and wherever the idea or thought occurs. By now you will have figured out, hopefully, that the key thing here is to find a format that works for you – that can be maintained, and does not end up gathering dust with only a few pages filled. This list needs to be your daily companion in all things.

Now let's discuss how to prioritise these items so that some actually get to be ticked off your to-do list as 'done' – never to return!

On a daily basis, everything often seems like a priority. To get to a prioritised to-do list, you need to focus first on your 'target self' personal vision objectives and take your priorities from there. If one of your main goals this year is, for example, to complete an MBA course, you might seek to commit, as a priority, to writing 500 words of your latest MBA essay every day.

What if you need to choose between two objectives? The key thing here is clarifying your thoughts on what is most important. 'But it's all a priority', I hear you complain in unison, in a more eloquent version of the *Night of The Living Dead*! Is it really, though? Ask yourself what can wait, really wait. There is a big difference between a priority and something that is important. Important stuff is important to do, but does it need to be done today, right now? The ones that you answer 'yes' for are the priority items to put at the top of your to-do list.

Using the Agile method, as we've covered (and will do so more in Chapter 10), we seek to group some of these things together into more concerted blasts of effort to really make some progress, but for now let's get some basic momentum on the daily practice we began to develop in this chapter. Think about the tasks you want to prioritise. You might use a few criteria for this:

- something that is a 'blocker', stopping you from progressing something else;
- something that is constantly on your mind ('I've just got to do that');
- something that would be a big achievement to get done;
- something that is scaring you to do;
- something that is unmotivating, but that you've committed to do for someone else.

Scroll through your to-do list and mentally (or actually, if you prefer) classify these. Some days you are going to feel like tackling a certain type of to-do, other days you can simply take your pick from the list. Try it – but choose the one you want to do least first!

I also sometimes think about my to-dos in terms of sizing. I try to, roughly, guess the 'size' of the bits of work on my to-do list by splitting them into 15-minute chunks of time. Most mornings, if I get my morning routine right, I wake up when I need to, drink my coffee and have my breakfast – making sure I've had the extra 15 minutes on top of that before I need to hit my desk. This hour gives me four chunks of 15 minutes, so I can do four quick tasks, or focus a full hour of mental strength on a more complex or longer task.

Using this methodology, think about how quickly you could complete the top three things on your to-do list if you gave them 100% of your attention every morning. Could you do them in a single morning? It's likely you could, but it'll take complete clarity of purpose and for you to allow yourself to put other priorities aside.

Once your first priority 'to-do' is successfully completed, it will most likely transform your attitude, and make it easier to start on the next one as well.

Every evening I ensure that I have a note of the most important task I need to do the next morning (if you are writing a book, it could be every morning!), and I'm clear on my minimum objectives. Every morning. If I nail the first one quickly, I will move onto number two and three on the list, but invariably I'll not get any further than that. But don't be hard on yourself – achieving a key objective daily is already building significant momentum for you. One or two a day means you could be hitting over 500 a year.

The key for me, and where I potentially do have a differing opinion from many advisors, is that I think you need to accept that not all of the tasks are going to be 'game-changers'. Sometimes the one task to do will be a personal admin item that is not exactly going to change your world, but might help remove a mental obstacle or key 'blocker' for you, and therefore achieve something significant the next day (or in the next task).

Try this tomorrow: prioritise some to-dos using the criteria I mention, and size them based on how quickly you've completed equivalent tasks. See how it works out, and reflect on it as part of your daily routine.

No	To-do list (prioritised in order of what will build most momentum)	What part of my 'target self' personal vision is this achieving?	Why am I prioritising this?	How long am I going to spend on this?	To do today or to be done tomorrow?	When will I review this (the retrospective at the end of the current sprint)?
1			It's a blocker to doing something else	15 minutes		
2			It's been on my mind every day	30 minutes		
3			It would be a big achievement	45 minutes		
4			It is scaring me	1 hour		
5			It is unmotivating, but I've said I'd do it for someone	2 hours		
6						
7						
8						
9						
10						

Steps to execute your plan every day

I spent days, weeks and months working through and testing ALL of the elements of this chapter. Implementing major change to your daily routine is really hard. Of the things I'm suggesting in this chapter – and I really found them all incredibly hard to do – I realised I spent too much time worrying about what other people need, I never gave any focus to figuring out what I needed. I was always thinking, planning, coming up with new ideas, new schemes, doing new things, but I never paused and reflected on 'why' and 'where' I was going. Pausing to reflect and do a 'retrospective' is a tough discipline. We always intend to do it in our work and personal lives more regularly, but it is hard to do in such a fast-paced world. However, by pausing and reflecting on 'why' and 'where' you are going, it really helps you keep aligned to your original vision.

Hopefully it's working for you too. By now you will have done:

Step	Things to do	Reflection and further builds
Step 1	Support your journey through daily visualisation of achieving your 'target self' personal vision.	Try to note afterwards how this has made you feel. Does focusing on your 'target self' motivate you? If not, reflect on why this might be.
Step 2	Create a daily routine that is yours, and try to keep to it every single day.	How does it feel having more structure in your daily life? Where else could you develop more healthy routines?
Step 3	Create a reflection list with 'themes' for how you want to be this year.	It is hard to follow through on this – life does indeed 'get in the way' sometimes, but try to remain consistent and catch yourself when you are not being consistent to your themes.

▶

Step	Things to do	Reflection and further builds
Step 4	Make a prioritised to-do list of the one, three or five things you need to do at any one time.	This is one of the most critical areas to master; it's also counter-intuitive to some extent, as surely doing more things is better? But, honestly, doing a few things very well will massively push you forward.
Step 5	Learn to love positive thoughts and to laugh at negative ones.	This is key. We all have darker moments, but try to find a bit of humour in them if at all possible – and don't forget to celebrate the good ones too!

How I personally broke through this

As we have covered, the concept of a mini daily stand-up where you go through your coming day and reflect on yesterday is essential – a consistent reflection on what you achieved yesterday, what you intend to do today and if you have any blockers. These are three crucial concepts that have really helped me unlock some meaningful progress for myself, and also unlocked my ability to 'begin' stuff. I'd like you to begin to think about this. Let's talk about it. Find a time you think will suit you, and make sure you say every day:

1 What am I going to do today?

2 What did I achieve yesterday?

3 What are my blockers?

There are lots of super-proactive outcomes from working through the elements in this chapter, and finding a mechanism from which you can actively give yourself 'credit' for completing something new or crucial is so useful to your self-esteem, and can help unlock so much about what we tell ourselves.

Look, I can't swear to have hit my daily routine seven times out of seven days every week since I began it in earnest, but I'd say, on average, that I have managed it six out of seven times. And honestly, it has transformed how I approach my life.

Also, I can't tell you the difference my 'walk out the door' list has made to reducing my daily stress levels!!!

If you want more

If this chapter has piqued your interest, you can find more resources, including videos and workbooks, at www.drgeraintevans.com

chapter 9

'L' – Less is more

There are so many distractions in life – from people, devices or advice on things that seem positive, but may derail you. So, where to begin? I will offer some inspiration and suggestions on how to prioritise ruthlessly in order to ensure your goals, strategies and projects deliver – and have a meaningful impact.

How others have broken through this

'One of the lessons that I grew up with was to always stay true to yourself and never let what somebody else says distract you from your goals.'

Michelle Obama

You might be thinking. . .

You say: 'There is so much to do, and I don't even know where to start.'

I say: 'You can't do everything all at once – chunk things up and pick one, any one.'

You say: 'But what if I miss out on something amazing?'

I say: 'You are more likely to miss something beautiful to you, if you are trying to see everything.'

Wow! Things are so busy, aren't they? So many projects, emails, phone calls to return, proposals to write, businesses to start, coffees, drinks and not to mention family, friends, the gym, and that cupboard you just never get around to sorting out. All things that suck time, energy and resources from you. Where do you start?

Saying 'no' is by far the hardest thing in the world but if we can learn to say it, nothing can stop us. Make 'no' your best friend. Like its close cousin, failure, 'no' is not actually a negative. It is a positive statement. It is a decision. It is not closing a door, it is choosing another path. 'No' is to be respected like no other word.

But, man, is it hard to say 'no'! So hard! 'I mean, maybe I could.' 'Let me see if I can fit it in.' 'Yeah, I can do this later, I guess.' 'Maybe I should?' 'What if I miss out on something good?' 'And what if I always say "no" to something, is that right? What if I'm closed to something amazing?'

Tough, isn't it? We are all together on this one, so let's spend some quality time on this. This chapter deals with the challenging topic of learning to say 'no' in a uniquely positive way, or using it as a force to challenge your preconceptions.

We'll discuss how being distracted and led by other people so often derails us. Let's learn to say 'no' to the temptation not to focus on what we know we need to do. We'll again work through some practical examples, ideas and frameworks for you to experiment with, and find your own relationship with 'no' – how and when you need to say it and how to deal with difficult conversations, unknowns and forks in the road.

As a skill, saying no is essential to unlocking your potential. Gurus and advisors often throw out quite confusing and contradictory stuff on this: learn to say 'no', or learn to do the opposite and say 'yes' to everything. No wonder people are confused. Let's explore each of these strategies, to see which one might resonate with you.

Learn to say 'no' to yourself

A really brilliant way to learn to say 'no' to yourself is a little controversial: try saying 'no' to more objectives as you progress through your sprints and months of work. Some experts will say to set a new goal for every one you have accomplished. For me, this is not the approach I found helped me as the months rolled by. You can totally disagree and do exactly that, of course, but let me explain why this is dangerous. I'm guessing that, like me, this is your first year of really trying to focus on a body of things you want to achieve. You've probably set short-term objectives before and tried to refocus, but this is bigger than that. By setting such a firm 'target self' personal vision, and the associated objectives and tasks you are now working though, you've taken on a lot – it's all very positive, hopefully, but you need to back yourself and follow through on what you are doing.

You can, of course, use your quarterly (or the frequency you desire) review to tweak your objectives and tasks if they no longer feel aligned to your overall vision, but don't forget this is a 'one-in/ one-out system' – you can switch things up, but the relative volume of the objectives and tasks should be equivalent.

You are also going to have some unexpected bumps in the road – events you could not predict. This is not being negative, this is being proactive – if you mentally prepare for these, they will not derail you as much as they might have. Do not get sucked into 'pre-worrying' about what you cannot control though – this is not at all what I mean here. I mean just 'know' that it's not going to always go smoothly, but also know you'll get back on the horse just as soon as you can. These bumps can blow up a series of sprints of activities before you know it – you might lose a whole month or more of your year to achieve your 'target self' personal vision. So, leave some slack and don't be tempted to keep piling things up.

Do one thing NOW

Although I want you to try not to overload your year with more objectives, do however make a note of anything new that might work as a future objective, and put it down as a candidate for a future year (it's been at least a few paragraphs since you've needed to create ANOTHER list, c'mon!).

Now, if it feels really pressing to address something, there is a mini-loophole on this. If you rapidly progress through *all* of the required work to meet your objectives, you can decide to do one of three things:

1 Start on another objective/set of tasks to 'get ahead' for next year.

2 Take a bit of time off and recharge (preferred option!).

3 Give yourself the 'luxury' of doing something unplanned, but that will positively contribute to your future 'target self'.

Interestingly, option 3 can throw up some very fun surprises. I've subsequently managed to achieve many things that I did not expect to do – including giving up drinking 10 cups of coffee a day, for example (just down to a few now!).

Say 'no' to distraction of all kinds

Something that you are completely, 100% justified in saying 'no' to is distraction; in fact, it is a mandatory requirement of achieving what you want to achieve. Think of fighting distraction as a personal search for minimalism in your life – you want fewer things bothering you, fighting for space in your mind, for your attention.

Stopping where you work distracting you

Sometimes, you need to create a mess in order to clear things up. Upon returning from a nice break a while back, before starting on this new way of working that I'm proposing in this text, I arrived at a scene in my home office that was a disaster! Wrapping paper, receipts, boxes, paperwork and flash drives. I looked at it and felt a bit despondent; it was demotivating to even think about getting motivated to clean it. Eventually, after much involvement from our good friend 'procrastination', I spent half a day cleaning it up but also reducing the amount of distraction. So, this meant having only the things I really needed on my desk – a monitor, a keyboard and mouse. Even my filing tray, and fun things such as action figures, were moved out of my line of sight. I gained a new energy from solving the mess, and organising it when I was ready. The key to beginning this clearing process is knowing when 'enough is enough', and that you are being distracted away from achieving what you want to achieve. So, if you are already at or over the 'disorganised' edge (or you can see it rapidly approaching on the horizon like a scene out of *Mad Max: Fury Road*), it is time to get organised. Your style might be being deliberately 'disorganised' of course – the 'creative' desk of mess maybe? Nothing wrong with this, as long as you can stay focused 100% of the time.

But what if we look at things in a different way? Take some action and try to do this in your immediate working environment now:

- Tidy your desk until it is all sorted (if it is really bad, consider making this part of an objective to 'be more organised' when you do a review!). Grab the old papers and sort, file or shred if you are never going to need them – the main thing is get them out of your eyesight.

- Now actually clean your desk – spray it with an eco-friendly cleaning agent of your choice, and please don't forget to also do your keyboard and mouse!

- When you rebuild your desk, as I did, take a moment to take stock – do you have the right set-up to make you comfortable? If you don't have a home office, do you at least have a proper office chair or are you sitting on a folding plastic one? Maybe it's time to get a proper ergonomic one. Sick of those wires everywhere? Cable-tie them together or tuck them away. Get a monitor if you are always hunched over your laptop. I also strongly suggest getting a lamp and putting it on your desk for some extra light.

- Even if the only available place to work is your kitchen table (nothing wrong with that – some of the greatest books and companies have been born out of the kitchen), you should always want to feel at least 'ready' when you sit there, and ideally even a little excited, motivated and inspired to get to work.

- In case it works for you, some people recommend hanging up pictures that help open up your mind and, if possible, try to sit in some natural light, with a view of the outdoors and maybe some indoor plants near you too! If you need to store a lot of paperwork and items, then consider getting a new shelf to put them on, with folders for things that make sense to you (perhaps colour-coded), or a filing cabinet – but remember to get the individual items out of your line of sight.

• If you don't have a kitchen table, there is always the couch (not with the TV remote nearby though, please) or your bed (watch your posture!), but really try to use these as a last resort, unless they are just 'the place' where you feel most comfortable and inspired. It's all about trying things and finding your own way.

Some experts would view this activity as being a bit of a delay tactic to not actually doing any of the stuff that will get you ahead and towards your goals, but I can't see a negative in reducing distractions in this way. If you are trying to balance family time among all of this, then a fun build on this is involving them in helping you do this as an activity.

Stopping devices distracting you

This next activity is to be done offline. If you have been ignoring your email inboxes for a long while, but they're becoming a bit of a 'splinter' in your mind, then turn off your Wi-Fi and consciously clean them all up offline, reply to the emails you really need to and file the old ones if you need to keep them, but try to delete what you can! If things are really bad, make this the only activity you do for a whole day. Ensure that you only send replies or create more emails if you are taking action towards achieving one of your objectives, or something that will eventually create a positive outcome for you – including sorting out a problem that's been on your mind or putting some positive energy into a relationship.

In terms of smart devices, you are trying to minimise their opportunities to distract you. We've already discussed how these are the kings and queens of distraction. I've encouraged you to put your phone on airplane mode when you are in bed and sleeping, and, to be honest, I'd really encourage you to keep it like that while you work through your to-do list or at any time you need to really focus on something. If you can't bear to put it on airplane mode, at least turn the screen upside down so you are not seeing all of those notifications popping up.

Stopping people distracting you

Sometimes nice things can distract. They may be well-intentioned, but they are things that really distract you. When someone needs something from you, they are probably coming from a genuine place – your help and advice is what they need – but this may not be what *you* need right now. You need to control your own agenda and workflow as much as possible, so when someone interrupts you, it's okay to say 'no' to them. There's no need to bite their head off, just gently explain that you are in the middle of something and ask if you can discuss it shortly (or when you know you'll be finished).

There is also another variant of this, where 'no' means 'yes, but just not right now'. You might not want to make a snap decision – the key is not to let it distract you. When someone asks for something, say these simple words: 'I'm really into what I'm doing, and I want to give you quality time and focus. Can you email/text me with some good times for you and we'll fix a time to really work through this?'

Test saying 'no' more often

This is just a practical tip to try in your life generally. You get a lot of opportunities each day to actually say 'no' – so many more than you probably realise if you are anything like me and seem to say 'yes' to most things in a well-intentioned way. Try saying 'no' if someone says 'sorry to interrupt, but have you got a minute?'.

Key to beginning to develop this behaviour is to develop some self-awareness. Recognise times when you could say 'no' but don't.

Test saying 'yes' when you'd ordinarily say 'no'

So many experts write about this one – doing the opposite to what you normally do. This is rocky territory, so let's take this slowly.

When we discussed the 'story' of ourselves, we may have recognised that we tell ourselves things like 'I can't do that', 'that is not me', or 'what will "they" think?'. This is the voice inside us that might tell us to say 'no' to something unexpected, something out of our comfort zone or just not what we'd ever expect us to be, say, go to, or do.

Consider these offers seriously and, again, don't be afraid to say 'no' if it feels like the right thing to do. However, listen to the voice deep down inside you – is this opportunity triggering something? Are you resorting to type and doing what you always do when you could actually try something new?

Learn to ask for more information when you are not sure

This is a crucial skill to learn and it can really help you navigate the waters of saying 'no', and recognising when you might be closed to a new opportunity to grow.

This is an area I've continually fallen foul of in my life. My instinct was always 'yes, great – let's do it', not pausing to think if this was right for me or if I was simply just trying to 'please' people as part of my own story.

There are a variety of ways to actually ask for more information. I know it can be hard for a lot of people to admit when they don't understand something, fearing it makes them look weak in some way (which is so not true – in fact, I think it's a sign of strength to do so), but there are a few tactics you can use. For example, if you are in a meeting and someone quickly goes over a topic that you do not understand, politely stop them and ask them to go over it again. If this makes you uncomfortable, you don't need to explicitly say 'I don't understand', just ask them to repeat it or 'go into more detail'. Another way to do this is in writing. If someone sends you something you don't fully understand, you can always express an interest in it and ask for more information from that person and thus get into a conversation about it. Ask questions – people love answering them!

Steps to execute your plan every day

Saying 'no' can become a really powerful force for good and change in your life if harnessed correctly. The good thing about 'no' is that it is really testable – you don't need to go 'all-in' like some of the things I'm suggesting in this text. However, in the case of the related topic, 'distraction', there is no compromise – when you are ready to commit to doing something, you need to avoid distraction at all costs. Fight distraction like the plague.

Step	Things to do	Reflection and further builds
Step 1	Create a 'next year' list for any objectives that you don't want to 'swap' for equivalent ones in this year.	What pattern are you seeing in this list? Can you see a change in your attitude to how much you can achieve in the future?
Step 2	Become aware of being distracted and build such distractions into a list you can refer to.	Have a personal plan on how to immediately refocus when distraction happens.
Step 3	Test saying 'no' five times this week.	How was that?
Step 4	Test saying 'yes' to one thing you would ordinarily say 'no' to.	How did it make you feel?
Step 5	If you are not sure, it is okay to say so and to ask for more information.	How did it feel to break a pattern of behaviour on this? Will you feel more comfortable asking next time?

How I personally broke through this

Thanks for surviving a whole section of this text on the 'no' word, as it can seem rather confusing advice on this front: learn to say 'no', don't say 'no', say 'yes' to the things you say 'no' to.

You need to practise saying 'no', like you practise going to the gym. How many times a day does someone come up to you and start a sentence with 'Am I interrupting?' or 'Could you just?' or 'Do you mind?'? And what is the first thing out of your mouth? Probably, if you are like how I used to be (and still suffer from sometimes), it will be: 'Sure. . . .' You've stopped, your flow is over! You have been nice, but where has it got you – or, really, the other person? Learn to give quality time by asking for it. I realised that often I was actually not helping by trying to help too eagerly. I also got better at finding other ways to say 'no'. For example, if it is not a good time for you to speak on something, try something to the effect of 'Sorry, I'm actually really focused, can we come back to this?', or faced with a choice you know you should not do, try 'Normally I would, but. . .' or 'I wish I could but I'm afraid. . .' . You may feel more comfortable with these type of nicer, slightly more polite phrases than the dreaded 'no'!

If you want more

If this chapter has piqued your interest, you can find more resources, including videos and workbooks, at www.drgeraintevans.com

chapter 10

—

'F' – Focus and failure

> ## How others have broken through this
>
> 'People think I'm joking when I say that whoever experiments the most in life wins. But I'm not. . . '
>
> Tai Lopez

This chapter will focus on embracing and handling failure, and learning from it in order to make massive progress. We are into a lot of deep learning now, and I am sure it's hard to retain focus even just working through these chapters. However, continued and renewed focus is the only way you can develop sustained momentum and also gain a greater understanding of yourself. We don't just need to rely on ourselves either – we can seek mentors to help us, and we need to learn to work in short bursts – or sprints – of activity to keep going, going and going!

Focus on creating a to-do list that works for you

We all know about the 'to-do' list thing – it rapidly becomes completely full, and therefore impossible to complete.

The main thing here is to avoid creating what I call a 'to-do list to-do list' – you know, 'I must put together a to-do list to put together a list of all the things I need to do'. If you need to do this, you've got too much to do!

There are many theories of productivity that can underpin how to handle this. The 'Ivy Lee Method', for example, was allegedly implemented in 1918 by Charles M. Schwab (then one of the richest men in the world), who loved to find an edge over his competition, and by consultant Ivy Lee (a successful businessperson and a key figure in the foundation of public relations). It's a long story, often told in endless blogs on the subject if you want to dive into them, but basically Mr Lee was invited to speak to Mr Schwab's top executives about how, through implementing a simple process, he could achieve peak productivity. At the end of each work day, he suggested writing down the six most important things needing to be accomplished tomorrow, prioritised in order, and definitely no more than six tasks allowed. He advised that you should concentrate only on the first task and work on it until it was done before moving on to the second task – repeating the same process every day.

So, what's so hard about that? Well, soon our to-do list turns into 10, 20, 50 bullets, right? We try to get to the bottom of the list, but we never do. We get new ideas, we add, we iterate, we expand. We are also, typically, terrible at estimating how long our lovingly documented tasks take, aren't we? One thing I found was that my first task of the day frequently took the whole of my morning slot to 'get it done', which of course had the effect of the to-do list rolling into tomorrow, and then likely the next day as well. It might be thought, therefore, that to-do lists actually allow us to avoid what's important, or what might create the most impact in our lives, and that, maybe, we use them to put off doing the things we don't want to do – the hard stuff.

In this context, the one thing on your list you should accomplish today is probably the one you don't want to do – it's the hardest one. By tackling it and getting on with it, you can absolutely change your day – it will be a weight off your shoulders. Getting on with it as soon as you finish the meditation/gratitude-exercise part of your day will really help you.

No	Prioritised to-do list
1	
2	
3	
4	
5	

No	Prioritised to-do list
6	
7	
8	
9	
10	

Many of the people writing on this subject don't always account for the complexities, emergencies and unexpected events that so often hit us in life. However, limiting the number of tasks you need to do in the first place is something that pretty much everyone agrees on.

Revisit your to-do list – what do you really need to get done today/tomorrow? What five things will really move you forward?

Do one thing NOW

We all love to plan to do a lot of things – the very spirit of this text is encouraging you to do just that! But I also urge you to be realistic in what you can do. Try to do five really meaningful things from your to-do list each day and watch how much progress you begin to make!

Learn to. . . test and learn

Did I read that right? Did I write that right? Yes! Okay, let's dive into this – what exactly does 'test and learn' mean? For me, I'd rather think in terms of 'testing' than having to get everything right every time! Test and learn is a concept that has sprung up from some of the marketing practices of retailers, financial services and other consumer-focused companies, and is connected to the previous chapters as it is a means by which you can freely try new approaches to getting stuff done. We don't need to get hung up on closely measuring the effect of a new change for now – let's just see how it feels and try some new stuff.

We've already worked out how to be more prepared, how to plan, not over-thinking or over-planning beforehand, getting started and then refining following reflection after you've begun. This is iteration – you are already doing it, so let's take it to the next level.

I think some of the best things you can do don't take very long. How many times have you put off doing something, big, small, interesting, banal, and then finally pulled yourself up on your bootstraps and done it? What is the overriding sensation you feel? Satisfaction? Probably not. It's more like 'huh, well that wasn't so hard after all'. Possibly you are also saying to yourself: 'You are an idiot. Why did it take so long?'

I have found that, in my life, I do everything in iterations, chunks and bursts of activities. Think more like Usain Bolt rather than a marathon runner. There's nothing wrong with running a marathon to get to your 'target self', but there is also nothing wrong with short bursts of intense activity to make rapid progress.

Another great thing about taking an iterative approach is that it is set up as an approach to support learning – sure you have a 'goal' for what you are trying to do, but, even working in short sprints, sometimes you won't get everything done. Some things you'll recognise you need to improve on. Let's get into more detail on this.

Think in sprints of activity

How others have broken through this

'Success is actually a short race – a sprint fuelled by discipline just long enough for habit to kick in and take over.'

Gary Keller

Within Agile, sprints or 'iterations' are essentially short periods of fixed time where work is broken down into a set of actions. These 'timeboxed' sprints are fixed to ensure that the rigour we've been applying is applied regularly – so no longer than one month and most commonly two weeks, then track progress and re-plan. The principal method of tracking is the same daily stand-up you've been doing (called daily scrums in Agile, and obviously with more team members than just you!).

Here is something I want you to begin to apply before whatever your chosen 'sprint duration' might be: start with something called 'sprint planning' – a specific event that aims to define a few things that are useful concepts that just might resonate with you.

Typically, you would develop a sprint 'backlog' – this is the concept of identifying the set of tasks/work you think you can do in that time period before you reach the end ('the sprint goal'). This work should inform the achievements of your 'target self' personal vision of yearly objectives. Each sprint ends with a sprint retrospective that reviews progress – to 'tick off' what you have done and also identify lessons you have learned and therefore improvements you can implement for your next sprint. Again, remember, you may not achieve in every 'sprint' you do, but that is okay – just LEARN from this! What did you fail to complete in the sprint? Next time you do it, use this lesson to reappraise your estimated forecast of what you think you can achieve.

If this feels natural and achievable, another Agile/scrum principle that might help you take things to the next level is its emphasis on creating (or 'shipping') a working product at the end of the sprint to show the work really has been done. In the case of software development, where this methodology has mainly come from, this usually means the product has been fully tested, integrated and documented. How to apply this? One extension to the basic planning of those tasks you feel it's possible to do within one sprint is to focus on grouping tasks together that sit logically with one another and, when combined and finished, constitute 'something' as completely done. This does not mean 'finished', of course, as much of your activity might take you the whole year to complete, but maybe a 'chunk' of something is done: a chapter of a book (or an essay!), for example; a new basic website that has a number of pages, all of the links work, all of the content is there, even if you know you are going to evolve it and create more pages in due course; or perhaps a social media account with content?

Another interesting concept to consider is the idea of picking objectives and tasks and doing some detailed thinking on their scope and nature, and if they can be split up or approached in a different way (called 'elaboration' in Agile). You might even choose to put some ideas back into your 'backlog' (the things you know you want/ need to do, but have not got to yet in a sprint).

I know that is a lot to take in, but the basic principles are pretty straightforward. Decide (according to the experiences of working on your objectives to-date and the general circumstances of your life) what your 'sprint' or iteration duration is going to be. I settled on two weeks after a lot of trial and error. Begin each one of these weeks by holding a more detailed daily planning session to identify which of your objectives you intend to tackle first, and the tasks you already know are inherent in that. Have a think whether the tasks are 'right' – can they be broken down further? Are there things, in retrospect, you might want to tweak and change? Are there any lessons from your regular review (I do mine quarterly, you might choose to do it more frequently) that you want to apply?

What's going well?

When you reach a natural pause point in your journey, at the end of each stretch of work, remember that you should do a retrospective. The best way to think of these is as the type of review you never actually end up doing at work – the campaign review you meant to do before you started on the next campaign or the end-of-quarter performance review that became more about filling in a set of PowerPoint slides rather than actual reflecting!

So, let's pick out the highlights of what you've done well in this first stretch of work (it might be a week, a month, but I'm guessing maybe it's more like six weeks for many of you). What went well?

Has the new routine bedded in well? How about the individual tasks against the objectives you set? How have they gone? If you are anything like me, a mix of 'easier than I expected' and a larger set of 'took me so long to do it' or 'did it, but really underestimated it' might be what you are thinking! This is totally to be expected. Keep a close eye on the things you are happy with as you progress.

Before you get too judgemental on yourself, I'm guessing you've managed to complete at least one thing, right? So, that's gone well? You've discovered a new podcast you love? Great! You smashed at least one objective and you are now already reaping the reward? Well done.

You've taken a step – a big step. Although that might be hard to connect with right now, you've proven to yourself that you can commit to something and follow through. Congratulations! (See, other people are giving you credit already!)

What's not gone so well?

Now let's dive into some of the more negative areas of the retrospective. Did you find any of the blockers we covered in Chapter 7 come back to haunt you and hinder your progress?

I suggest re-reading your 'splinter list' to see if it is any of these culprits. Remember, you OWN these people, things or feelings – they are on one of your (my?!?) lists! Seriously – I know it is hard, but even being able to connect those splinters to a lack of progress on a specific task is an incredible breakthrough, isn't it? You now know why you are stuck or maybe don't follow through as you'd like to? That is pretty awesome, isn't it?

Okay, so with the 'reasons' clearly in mind, now delve a little deeper. What is going on overall for you? Apart from the 'task' level of doing stuff, how is it feeling? Are you embracing the learning experience as well as the 'doing stuff' bit of it?

Have you reviewed your 'day plan' and tried tweaking things, or just persisted with it? I love the commitment, but if something in particular is just not clicking (not in a 'Wow! It's tough to do X' kind of way, but in a truly 'I'm not happy with the way it is working out at all' way), then try to tweak it – try a little more or a little less and see where it gets you. Do not see addressing things that have not gone well as a negative or failure.

Better 'quality' time management

How others have broken through this

'Think about your job. How much of your time is wasted while you're waiting for someone else to finish their work, or for information to be delivered, or because you're trying to do too many things at once? Maybe you would rather be at work all day – *me*, I'd rather be surfing.'

Jeff Sutherland,
Scrum: The Art of Doing Twice the Work in Half the Time

When it comes down to it, no matter how much you plan and 'get ready', you've got to DO SOMETHING that gets you closer to your 'target self' personal vision. This means getting in front of your laptop, tablet, typewriter or notebook and working to complete things. Even if you are following my suggestion of making this only three to five key actions each day, you still run the risk of running over time and getting distracted.

So, in case it's useful, here are a few tips to support your daily practice – and to make sure you maximise the time you do devote to those development tasks that support your 'target self' personal vision.

According to Tony Schwartz of 'The Energy Project', we generally don't handle our days very well. For example:

- Only one out of three people takes a real lunch break – that does not mean eating at your desk while working, by the way!

- A single microbreak (of thirty seconds to five minutes) can improve your mental performance by an average of 13%.
- As humans, we naturally move from having full focus and energy to devote to a task to physiological fatigue every 90 minutes.
- The most productive people actually spend 52 minutes working, followed by a 17-minute break.

Interestingly, also according to Schwartz, multi-tasking creates 7–9% more errors in your work. So, how can we apply some of this? The Pomodoro Technique, a time management method developed by Francesco Cirillo in the late 1980s, suggests:

- decide on the task to be done;
- set the timer to 25 minutes;
- work on the task until the timer rings;
- take a short five-minute break;
- repeat four times;
- take a 15–30-minute break!

What do you think? Does this connect with you? If so, guess what – try it! As distraction is your enemy in many cases, this allows you to focus on not being distracted as there is a timer on you!

However, my suggestion is to make this contextual and to plan for when you focus on tasks. I would recommend also grabbing 'mini opportunities' to do substantive work over and above any time you might set aside daily – for example, during your commute before you 'begin your day job'. These can be great times to focus. However, a warning – I literally wrote this passage on a Thameslink train to London and I missed my stop!

Lessons learned from this: I got locked into a real 'flow' state for all the right reasons, but got that wrong outcome because I did not plan my work within a defined period of time. I mean, I could have set an alarm on my phone or something at least! I still made my 10am meeting on time, but I was a little sweatier, a little less focused, had not gone through my resumé of what I wanted to get out of it, and winged it a little more than I would have liked.

Understanding urgent vs important

Wow! This is a good one! The Eisenhower Matrix (pictured) offers a framework for judging a common issue when actually doing tasks – what is urgent to do versus what is simply important.

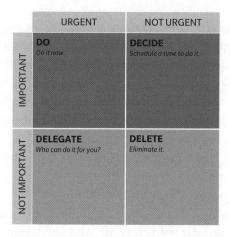

The Eisenhower Matrix https://luxafor.com/the-eisenhower-matrix/

For what it's worth, my order of tackling this list is as follows:

1 Urgent/Important – as it says on the diagram, do it now, and do it FIRST in your daily task list.

2 Not Urgent/Important – decide if you want to schedule time to do it. This is a tough one – I always ask 'why' it is not urgent, as often a crucial future piece of work is hidden in these lists! Will it become urgent and important if not addressed? For me, this would be second on the 'to-do' list.

3 Not Urgent/Not Important – this is a potential 'delegate' task according to this methodology, but in personal terms, these are often more 'important' than they appear at face value, so do consider if you can do it yourself, or delegate it only if you have a resource you can trust to deliver it for you. This would be third on the 'to-do' list.

4 Not Urgent/Not Important – as it says on the tin, delete!!
   Seriously, you need to minimise the things you are focused on so
   this would be one easy one to remove.

Failure is not failure

The dictionary definitions of failure are hard to get away from –
literally meaning a lack of success, or the neglect or omission of
expected or required action. Some of the synonyms for it are
equally pernicious: defeat, frustration, collapse, floundering, misfir-
ing, coming to nothing, or falling through. An alternative definition
describes failure as when you don't comply with the basic rules.

Wow! So, no wonder we are all so scared of it. Time to reframe
what failure is – and what it is for you.

It is okay to not get it right first time.

It is okay to not get it right the second time.

In fact, it is okay if it takes you a very long time to get there – this
is such a valuable learning opportunity. It has made you stronger.
You'll not do things in the same way again, will you? You'll try
something new ('test and learn'), you'll do it slightly differently –
you might even end up doing it better.

How others have broken through this

'I have gotten a lot of results! I know several thousand things
that won't work.'

Thomas A. Edison

Remember what we discussed in the work on blockers and
unleashing your energy? No one owns what you do, and no one
is judging you apart from yourself (and if they are, that is their
problem to handle, not yours). There is no need to see your failure to
do something as a failure. Instead it is an opportunity to grow, so, as
usual, laugh, chin up and let's go again on the next sprint.

Doing things in manageable boxed-in stretches of work is a game-changer. It stops the temptation to commit to a huge volume of tasks, in a never-ending series of weeks of trying – and we've all been there, I am sure. Reviewing, really reviewing, how things are going rather than just ploughing into new tasks was an extremely hard habit for me to establish as a regular part of my life. It's not that I *never* looked back and did this, but I could not say, hand on heart, that I did it every time, or implemented what I learned. Having better task discipline is also key and multiplies your productivity. As for viewing failure as a negative – absolutely not, never again, no way.

Consider getting some mentors

How others have broken through this

'Alone we can do so little; together we can do so much.'

Helen Keller

The idea of needing mentors to help us has been well written about – however, so few of us actually have a formal (or informal) one. Why is this? Again, I believe this is due to a focus on what is 'weak' about needing help. We feel we should know it all. We should not need help. Why can't we just find the strength within ourselves? For me, the crucial element here is that we need people we can trust to help break through this extremely limited thinking. Why should we know the answers? Why should we not need help?

Ask yourself if you know all the answers – really ask yourself if you believe this to be true? I'm guessing 99% of you can accept you don't. It is totally okay for this to be the case. In fact, practise embracing that idea for a second – literally say out loud 'I don't know everything. I need some help – and that's okay'. Tried it? How many of you hesitated? I know I did when I first began to do this. In fact, the first few times I literally could not say the words – I was struggling against the notion that I could not do everything I needed to do to achieve all of my goals myself. If I just focused a little more, just tried a little harder, it would all work out. The truth is, focusing and working harder is a huge part of the puzzle, but we need guidance and support too.

So, just go with me on this – accept you need help and that you don't know all of the answers (or maybe not even some of the answers!), so getting someone to help you figure them out might be useful.

I define my mentors who help me with my personal focus in three ways:

- virtual mentors
- physical mentors
- visualised mentors.

Virtual mentors

We have covered a lot on reading, learning and consuming video content to help you achieve your aims (see Chapter 4), but to get you in the right mindset I encourage you to identify early on those people you connect with who could be your 'virtual mentor'. They are not necessarily someone you personally interact with (although many motivational gurus do offer coaching and 'masterclasses' on their particular philosophy), but will be someone you can tune into and use as a mentor. This could be through learning from their experiences or how they built their own success story. As a side note to this, I also use some people as an example of what 'I don't want to be'. I don't labour too long on their content as I think this is a somewhat risky strategy as it leads to the dark side of hate and negativity – but it is useful sometimes to have a visible emblem of what you *don't* want.

Physical mentors

Physical mentors are people you can meet with in your real life (albeit you might do so over a video call) to work through what you are trying to achieve. They may take a number of forms. For example, some people will connect with general 'coaches' who are able to work with them on their overall attitude and mindset and be a sounding board. This is particularly useful for those of you who struggle to share with others. Other people might want someone who has literally 'done' what they aspire to do, to be able to really interrogate how they did it and what keeps them there. Some people will want both types of support – I do, for example – as it helps give you a variety of different perspectives and input. I've included some resources for finding a coach in the 'Further reading' section of this text, but finding a mentor who is already 'doing what you want to do' can sometimes be a bit more challenging. However, in my experience, people are actually more approachable than they may at first seem and will be willing to help within agreed parameters. The prominence of social media also means that people are more searchable and reachable than ever – all you need to do is pluck up the courage to send a polite instant message to them along the lines of: 'Hi X, my name is Y. I am a great admirer of what you've achieved. I am looking for a mentor to help coach me to get to a similar place in my own career. Would you be willing to explore this? If so, please let me know the best way to arrange a time to speak.' Copy this and give it a try!

Visualised mentors

To begin to develop a strong 'target self', or manifestation of your hopes, dreams and desires, have a think about the people you are aware of (either living or passed) who are an obvious inspiration to you – people you don't need to think too hard to come up with but just instinctively think of when you visualise achievement and being more like the person you want to be, or the life you want to create. Make a note of this person. Write down what it is about them you like – what you want to have. Recognise what language you are using – what 'things' are important? Just free associate and write a stream of consciousness. As hard as it is, don't censor yourself – this is just for you. Don't write what you think is politically correct or what would be an accepted norm. If you desire the physical or financial things they have, put this down. If you like who they are and what they stand for, put this down.

The key for all of these mentor types is to teach yourself to receive constructive feedback and, in some cases, criticism. Again, as hard as it is, we need to reframe criticism as an additional way to improve and progress, not as a mark of failure. Consider failure to be something that can be a friend to you – to help you learn. Areas of weakness can become strengths – you just need to be aware of them to improve on them. So, again, if one of these mentors identifies directly or implicitly a 'fault' or weakness in you, see this as a fantastic opportunity to make a positive change. There is, however, a significant health warning that comes with this: if you ever feel truly judged to the point that deep down inside you don't think the person you are being mentored by is coming from an open and honest place, trust your instincts and move on to a more positive support system.

How others have broken through this

'It's not how far you fall, but how high you bounce that counts.'

Zig Ziglar

Steps to execute your plan every day

Moving my working life into a series of 'sprints' of activity, followed by a 'stop' and period of reflection every two weeks, has really helped me achieve my objectives. You choose what works best for you, but I found that only one week, while building moments, never quite seems long enough to cope with the unexpected challenges life throws at you!

Remember – the key is to become comfortable iterating things – do it in chunks with short-term goals, then review. Then repeat, and repeat!

Step	Things to do	Reflection and further builds
Step 1	Start each day (or end each day if you prefer) with a mini stand-up, asking yourself the three key questions we've discussed in this text: what did I accomplish yesterday, what am I aiming to do today and what is stopping (or 'blocking') me from progressing?	Take note of anything that is consistently getting in your way of achieving what you set out to do.
Step 2	Adopt a 'test and learn' attitude to progressing your objectives and tasks.	Remember, failing is all part of progressing – you need to not do things perfectly to learn how to improve things!
Step 3	Decide what 'sprint' duration makes sense to you (e.g. two weeks) and begin to plan activity in these chunks of time.	Remember, the objective of the sprint is to try to 'complete' as many things as possible in the allotted time.
Step 4	Focus on quality time management to ensure you are focused 100% on a given task.	Note down the reasons you are getting taken off course when trying to focus – does something come up again and again that you could address?
Step 5	Decide your urgent/important criteria and order your daily three to five tasks in that way – ruthlessly, with no exceptions!	Focus on reflecting on what you achieved yesterday (give yourself credit, or a pep talk!).
Step 6	Approach a potential mentor.	Write down the traits of someone you admire.

Step	Things to do	Reflection and further builds
Step 7	Consider 'telling some-one' about your current goals and intent if you feel it may help you maintain momentum.	Reflect on this if it is a change of attitude – how do you feel about creating a new degree of accountability?

How I personally broke through this

As with everything in this text, I've road-tested all of the things I'm suggesting, and I too found many of them to be a big challenge to do. My main realisation from this work was how little I had given myself permission to fail, or to be comfortable with the notion I cannot get everything right first time and that I am not perfect, basically! The sooner I embraced the fact I did not know all of the answers, and that I needed to learn through doing and also seeking the help of other people, the sooner I made massive, massive progress.

So, if you've done everything I've suggested, you will now have said out loud: 'it is okay that I don't know all of the answers, and can't do this all by myself'.

If you want more

If this chapter has piqued your interest, you can find more resources, including videos and workbooks, at www.drgeraintevans.com

chapter 11

——

You can do this

How others have broken through this

'We just have to remain faithful and humble and helpful while we wait on our own personal breakthroughs.'

Jason Mayden

Well done (and thanks so much!) for getting this far. I hope – and believe – you are doing great, and I hope the positive changes you are making in your life are impacting you and improving the sense of wellbeing and momentum in your life. I'm guessing (and hoping) that if you've been working through the actions, you are a good few weeks/months in and are seeing some changes, or if you are reading this on a plane in one go, you have already noted many things you are going to return to and implement.

For those of you who have not taken any of the steps I've suggested, I really urge you to do so, and to come back to this section of the text at a later date. However, I also hope that some of the thinking in this chapter might unlock something for those of you who are still stuck.

So, you've made good progress, hopefully have some great daily practices working and are even saying 'no' to things. Wow! You are really doing it now. With your next and possibly one of the biggest years of your life and its exciting activity to get you even more 'ahead' already looming, I want you to come back to your original vision. When we went through this activity at the start, I asked you to spend only a little amount of time thinking about the longer-term future. This was a deliberate strategy on my part. I wanted you to try focusing on positive changes and getting going – on building momentum.

- -

You might be thinking. . .

You say: 'I know I need help, but I don't know where to start.'

I say: 'Give yourself permission to ask for help – this is an admission of strength, not weakness.'

- -

You've proven that you can achieve things – you can change. I didn't want you to get stuck in wishing for a future that seems so far away and then get frustrated or, worse, not take a step due to not knowing where to start or worrying that you might fail.

So, here are some additional ideas on how to keep building more and more AND MORE momentum. Reflect on the following.

Be consistent with the person you want to be

A big focus for me this year has been concentrating on being inwardly and outwardly the person I want to be – so it is a consistent and authentic 'me' that I and others experience. Let me explain through examples. This may mean that when I catch myself saying an acerbic comment (perhaps when someone cuts me up in traffic), I try to catch myself before a volley of abuse comes out of my mouth, or even into my mind.

There are a number of other cool things to try here too.

Cheerfulness and warmth

Tony Robbins talks about this at length, and how it is not the same thing as being 'happy' *per se*, but that it's a great way to project a warm, positive feeling about yourself when you walk in a room. So, when you enter, try smiling, laughing and being warm to the people in it – you'll be amazed at the results.

Positivity

Positivity for non-positive people is hard, I know. Since I've been focused on being more positive in my life, sometimes I catch myself thinking, 'Wow! I've not been stressed for a while'. This is largely due to the daily practice of having a positive mindset. Positivity is also a very attractive, infectious quality – we all need positive people in our lives (see Chapter 5) and like to be with people who can get us through the tough times.

Passion

Passion is also an incredible thing to demonstrate. If you love doing something – really love it, and show it – then let others in on how you are feeling and ask them what they are passionate about as well. You'll be amazed by the effect.

Share more and be okay with the result

How others have broken through this

'Not all of us can do great things. But we can all do small things, with great love.'

Mother Teresa

Share more and get less hurt when someone does not automatically say exactly the right thing. Sharing equals slightly less frustration.

Be curious

It's funny how we lose our curiosity as we grow older. If you speak to any child they have it in abundance – asking all the 'why' questions. Try doing that about your own life, goals and interests!

Praise others

How others have broken through this

'You need to be aware of what others are doing, applaud their efforts, acknowledge their successes, and encourage them in their pursuits. When we all help one another, everybody wins.'

Jim Stovall

When was the last time you gave someone credit? Told someone you respect them, appreciate or even love them – really love them? Try it, it might make you love yourself more.

Praise yourself

Go on, pat yourself on the back for something you did well – or even just did. No one, absolutely no one, is going to do it for you on a daily basis.

Really listen for praise from others

Listen, please listen, to the compliments when you get them. You do get them, really you do, but don't phase things out. Take a second to absorb the compliment, don't just allow it to be 'white noise'.

Don't forget to have a little fun

> # How others have broken through this
>
> 'For me, play is highly important, so I schedule it in.'
>
> Preston Smiles

Try to make sure you have a little fun, okay? However, key to this is to schedule it in as much as is possible. Spontaneous fun is great, but it's amazing how keen we are to timetable things we are not super-motivated to do, but don't do it for those things that we enjoy!

Master humility

Humility is an essential human quality in my view. However, humility gets an incredibly bad rap from a lot of people. A bit like its friend 'help', it sometimes (or a lot of the time) gets associated with a sense that you are not a true winner – you are not ruthless enough. We see a lot of people in boxing, for example, demonstrating what can be seen as incredible degrees of self-confidence in their actions. From Muhammad Ali to Floyd Mayweather to Conor McGregor, they all purport to be the greatest of all time, all of the time. In their cases, it's hard to argue – but they are not in the normal 99.9% of the population. They are people who need to believe to an extreme level, so they can survive.

What is not so often spoken about of these people, however, is their support network. It's true they possess an incredible inner self-belief as a starting point, but they have a plethora of experts and specialists surrounding them. From trainers, to nutritionists, to business managers and assistants, they rely on a network of people to help them be the best they can be.

This takes humility in my view. They would never characterise it as such, I imagine, but they recognise that in order to achieve, to keep achieving and do things that no human has done before, they need help.

This is true for us as well. We need to accept that we don't know all the answers. We aren't happy with where we are at the moment. We don't have all of the skills we need. We haven't acquired the knowledge that we need in order to be where we want to be. But we might be able to think about a new future.

Be okay with not knowing all the answers

How others have broken through this

'Teamwork begins by building trust. And the only way to do that is to overcome our need for invulnerability.'

Patrick Lencioni

Okay, before you get into the next set of objectives, sprints and tasks to work on and try, we need to address something else about what might be your present mindset and how it might be contributing to your present situation. According to Carol Dweck, writer and researcher at Stanford University, in her book *Mindset*, people have one of two types of mindset – a fixed mindset or a growth mindset – which will define many of the characteristics critical to a person's success.

People with a fixed mindset believe their personal traits and qualities are 'fixed' and cannot be changed. This includes assumptions that things such as intelligence and talents are natural, rather than being able to be developed and improved. Crucially, they also believe that talent alone leads to success, not hard work and effort.

People with a growth mindset possess the belief that their talents and intelligence can be grown and developed through learning over time and through acquiring new experiences. This also supports their belief that their efforts have an effect on and eventually contribute to their future success, ultimately leading to higher achievement.

Interestingly, according to Dweck, those with a fixed mindset often want to appear as intelligent and talented and greatly fear the inverse – not appearing to be that person to others! In a growth mindset, people embrace that they are not the finished article yet and are happy to be seen to be inquisitive about acquiring knowledge to fulfil their potential.

The key to these mindsets is the concept of it being 'okay to not know all of the answers' yet, but to absolutely believe you can develop anything you need to get them through growing your learning and therefore your intelligence over time. No matter who you are, your brain has the ability to grow and adapt throughout life, and is actually highly stimulated by new experiences, situations and environments. The idea of fixed beliefs can be a huge limiting factor. We've all been there on this, so don't beat yourself up about it. I am sure you have tried new things before, and maybe, ultimately, they didn't work for you. To begin making positive changes in your life, it's important that you believe you can change. However, crucially, it's also okay to recognise that you can improve on areas where you feel you have any weaknesses, any bad habits you'd like to eliminate. It is okay that you have not managed to improve them yet, but get ready as you really are about to.

First of all, acknowledge and embrace your weaknesses – write them down. Don't fear them, as you are about to significantly improve on how you handle them. Don't do this with a heavy heart, just list them without judgement. Next, look at them and change your focus – don't judge yourself. View them as a set of challenges that are, in fact, massive opportunities for you to learn about and improve yourself in new and exciting ways. Give yourself permission to do exactly that – but without judgement of yourself.

Let people in

How others have broken through this

'One piece of log creates a small fire, adequate to warm you up, add just a few more pieces to blast an immense bonfire, large enough to warm up your entire circle of friends; needless to say that individuality counts but teamwork dynamites.'

Jin Kwon

Clearly a lot of what we've discussed in this chapter – opening up your heart and head to help – is going to take you out of your normal comfort zone. Once you are ready to stop avoiding challenge and instead embrace it, you also need to consider how you will keep yourself on track and develop accountability for your progress, learning and growth.

Your mentors will be fulfilling a crucial role in terms of supporting a 'no-judgement' attitude to your progress. They should be objective and able to provide constructive criticism with your best intentions in mind.

A sticky subject to navigate next is the extent to which you 'let people in' to your new journey and share what you've embarked on. Even by completing the steps in the first couple of chapters of this text you are already progressing significantly, but you are still relatively alone. Your mentor relationship, if with a real person, is typically going to be occasional, not on a day-to-day basis. So, some people find it better to let in a few people close to them on what they are doing. This operates on two levels – one is simply to have someone to 'share' what you are doing with and to feel like you are not alone in your challenges. The other level is to make yourself more accountable for your actions – having a visual or metaphoric representation and reminder that you need to keep going, even if things get tough.

For some, these people will be an immediate partner, best friend, parent(s) or a close family member. They will be someone you feel completely confident in confiding in often, and who will be able to help you proactively during your journey. There is something really liberating about openly admitting what you are trying to do – vocalising it can really make it come alive for a lot of people. It's a powerful way to build intent and action in the right hands. Accountability can be helpful when your accountability partner is a friend.

However, in order to be balanced, I need to flag an alternative view on this concept – where people who are trying to help might, inadvertently (or in darker scenarios, deliberately), try to stop you achieving your goal. Consequently, some scientific researchers and commentators suggest *not* telling anyone of your plans and goals. I think it's really worth diving into detail on this, as I want to tackle potential blockers for you head-on. Well, if making change in your life was easy, texts like mine would not exist! So, let's explore some of the problematic areas in a little more detail.

Peter Gollwitzer and his team from NYU published research in 2009 that suggested that sharing your goal publicly could potentially make you less likely to do the work to achieve it. Their study of law students, measuring the most committed members of the class to making the most of their educational opportunity, saw them split into two groups and asked to complete a questionnaire.

The first group was asked to confirm that the answer they had circled (i.e. that they had high commitment to achieving the best possible results on their course) was what they had intended to choose. The second group, however, understood that their responses were to be anonymous. Both groups then worked on a legal case. However, the first group spent less time working on their case than the second group. The researchers concluded that when someone is brought into your goal, that social recognition and connection to your identity is 'a reward' that may then cause you to reduce your efforts – the students in the first group felt, in their minds, that they had already 'achieved' their aim in some way due to the researchers' acknowledgement of their answers. For me, however, this is a generalisation, as I feel that connection to what we are doing is an essential step in forming a new identity. If we structure our goals and objectives in specific ways (as we learned in Chapter 6), it is pretty clear that we are 'not there yet' – but letting someone in should not affect this, despite the interesting conclusions of this study.

There are multiple counterpoints to this discussion. For example, Tom Bilyeu (co-founder of Impact Theory) has said, 'When someone doesn't believe in you, that's the single greatest gift they can give you'. This is an interesting notion. Sometimes, proving people wrong is a fantastic way to achieve goals. We've all been there – we let someone into something and instead of support, we get derision. We all know what it is like to not be believed in – so, in some ways, you've got nothing to lose!

Seriously, I know this is a tough point. Decide consciously the extent to which you are going to let people in to what you are doing (or not), but before you do it, the main action is to think through what you are looking for, and how you are going to react if you get what you are looking for, or do not. That way, whatever happens, I hope you can derive some positive growth and challenge from the interaction. If you choose not to 'let anyone in' I totally understand that – if this is the case, then having mentors is even more important because, as we've concluded, you are amazing, but you can't do this alone.

Help someone else whenever you can

How others have broken through this

'It is literally true that you can succeed best and quickest by helping others to succeed.'

Napoleon Hill

A lot of what we've discussed so far is rightly focused on how you are going to help yourself. However, to bring some balance, I also want you to consider how you could be helping other people as well.

When you develop a strategy to help other people, it also helps you understand yourself in a whole new way, so let's really try to embrace this point. A lot of writers consider this to be an essential part of your evolution as a person, but for me, finding ways to help others really helped me focus on what I needed to do. I feel that finding a proactive way to help someone else is a mandatory concept to adopt while you focus on opening up your heart and ego to receiving help from others.

What I like about this is the balance. To use a *Star Wars* metaphor, and to quote Luke Skywalker, this life of ours is 'so much bigger' than just us, and while I'm advocating spending a whole lot of time focusing on improving yourself and your situation, I also think that crucial to this is helping others, to ensure they are benefiting from your journey too.

There are a number of practical ways to actually do this – see what resonates and do one or all of them (but do at least one!). If the 'OMG, I know this already' radar is going off in your head, ask yourself this: if you are doing some of these already, could you do more?

1 Choose a new charity you believe in as a cause, and whom you want to support whenever you can. What do you want to help them with? What could you give? Your time, your skills, your experience, or lending a hand when they need it? Could you fundraise for them more proactively – perhaps run a 5k or get your head shaved (but don't try to do both at the same time!). If everyone did this, what a difference it would make.

2 For other charitable areas you are keen on, but perhaps not so ready to get 'hands on' with, set up a direct debit to pay a set amount each month. This takes about 20 minutes to do, from the point of searching the internet, finding a charity you like the look of, going to their 'donate' page and setting something up. If each of you reading this put even a few pounds towards a charity it would literally transform the world and end all kinds of poverty and issues once and for all – you can do this on most major e-commerce websites by ticking a box at the checkout to give to a charity. Your work colleagues are sure to be regularly asking for help on a whole host of requests for a charity donation. You literally have no excuse.

3 Who can *you* mentor and support? Is there anyone in your life you could help using one of your skills, or just be a positive support to? While I'd encourage you to always try to help when someone asks, and to choose carefully when to do so uninvited, do look for opportunities to help. Who do you see that you wish you 'could do more to help' – have you actually asked them if they want help?

Do one thing NOW

Spend one hour now making an impact. Sign up to some charity direct debits, choose a partner on Amazon or eBay, or just give what you can. I spent one hour, one whole hour, googling a bunch of charities I was interested in, setting up a simple direct debit or PayPal payment and then, well, then I'd done it – I'd begun. Once you've begun, it's amazing how often you have small chances to give. If you can automate it, you'll be making such a difference to this planet.

See things through

Okay, so you've got a set of actions you are pursuing. We've discussed how to approach other areas of your life with a different energy, and you've done a bit of a reset. I'm guessing by now you've done a stretch of progressing your objectives as well. You've hopefully also made some tweaks to your daily routine that are benefiting you, and hopefully some tweaks to the relationships you have with family and friends, and that you are firing on all cylinders and in more fulfilling ways. Again, well done – take a moment to practise your 'give myself credit' routine!

So, here comes another hard part of this journey: following through. I want you to think about the remainder of the year exactly as you've just done – a set of blocks of time, where you broadly plan a set of tasks against one of your objectives and look to deliver progress against them on a daily basis, after which you do a full retrospective.

Now you need to develop a framework to deliver the remainder of your year. Begin by thinking and working in fixed blocks of time, or 'sprints' of activity, that feel logical to you, to really continue to deliver meaningful progress against the objectives you've got in your new 'target self' personal vision.

As well as focusing on what you need to achieve each day in your 'daily stand-up', which I hope you are living and breathing now ('What did I achieve yesterday? What do I want to achieve today? And what is blocking me from doing it?'), I now want to extend this concept to a more macro level and think in terms of setting up what you need to do in the next fortnight or week or month. (You choose the timeframe – if you are not sure, I'd suggest a fortnight as it's pretty easy to get derailed in a week sometimes but two weeks gives you a fighting and realistic chance to catch up where you have to!)

I also want you to get used to applying some of the principles of 'life-long' learning, and realise that we are essentially testing and learning as we go along. By taking this attitude (the growth mindset we discussed previously), everything helps us progress towards our goal and realisation of our 'target self'. We will inevitably 'fail' to do some things we set out to do and, guess what, that is awesome. Awesome? Yes, let's embrace failure as crucial to our progress.

Any changes you are making are so positive – any progress you make is an achievement. So don't stop now, keep going!

How I (continue to) break through this

I hope all I have written is useful – honestly, if you do implement it, it will change your life. But if you only do one thing, please, please find someone you can talk openly to during the next year. You will need to find incredible internal resources to get through the trials and tribulations any and every year presents, let alone one where you are looking to do things differently, but you won't be able to do it all alone.

Achieving growth is tough, so having a coach, a mentor or friend/family member by your side is going to be key.

Remember, no judgement of yourself, and ask for no judgement from them – just support, encouragement and constructive feedback.

If you want more

If this chapter has piqued your interest, you can find more resources, including videos and workbooks, at www.drgeraintevans.com

chapter 12

Some closing
thoughts

So, how has it been working through all of these ideas and 50-odd thousand words? Easy, tough, enjoyable, motivating, daunting – perhaps all of those things? Hopefully not boring anyhow! Don't worry, making some meaningful changes in your life is exactly about balancing things that have all of those traits, pretty much constantly.

Remember, you are amazing. Keep telling yourself you are amazing. Tell others they are amazing too – and then you can all do just about anything, anything at all.

By getting to the end of this, and hopefully doing a lot, or all, of the 'one things' I've suggested to take you forward, you are now beginning to deliver on becoming your true 'target self'. Progress in life comes through action, so keep taking it. There will be many more ups and downs, and maybe some key forks in the road where you will need to make big decisions, but keep going. You *will* arrive where you are meant to be – at your chosen destination.

If you have made it this far and are still considering if following the advice in this text is the right thing for you, I understand and respect that. All I ask is that you just try to do the first thing I proposed – which is to please free your mind to the possibility of booking some quality time for yourself like it's the most important meeting of your life. Even if you can only spare an hour, even if you aren't ready to do the full timeline and projection thing, even if you don't want to build a 'target self'. Please still take some time to yourself to reflect (and make sure you have some paper to hand just in case you get into the ideas. . .). You never know what might happen.

Next to this, I urge you to keep connected with people about how you are feeling – you need to let people in no matter what you are thinking, and seek help if you are just not feeling right.

So, truly and deeply, I thank you so much for considering my thoughts and feelings in this area. As I've mentioned throughout, there is a massive amount of content and thinking in this space, and this text is fully intended to be a jumping-off point for further learning and motivation in your life. All I've set out to do is to help you get started doing some of the things that will help you in discovering and achieving your life goals, whatever they may be.

If I haven't said so already, also a massive thanks to those closest to me for all of their support in allowing me to create this text, and for supporting me in my period of rest, reflection and re-energising in my own life.

Good luck, and let me know how you are getting on!

Dr G x

Your new list of nine assets

I appreciate I've gone over a lot of new things in this text. By now you should have the following list of assets to help provide some structure for what is next for you.

No	Type of asset	What it is for	Where did we discuss this?
1	A single place (or list)	A single place (or list) where you are committing to capture all your thoughts, ideas and actions.	Chapter 1
2	A written, long-term 'target self'	A symbol of where you are going and who you want to be.	Chapter 2
3	A 'target self' vision	A vision for the next period you are doing detailed planning for – whether it's the next 12 days, 12 weeks or 12 months.	Chapter 3
4	A set of SIMPLE objectives	A set of objectives to achieve your 'target self' personal vision.	Chapter 6

No	Type of asset	What it is for	Where did we discuss this?
5	A daily journal	A place to capture reflections and to journal on a daily basis.	Chapter 8
6	A daily prior-itised 'to-do' list	A list of daily tasks set out in order of priority and urgency.	Chapter 8
7	A morning list	A checklist of things to watch out for or do each and every morning.	Chapter 8
8	An evening list	The same as a morning list, but to be done at the end of the day if that is your more productive time.	Chapter 8
9	A 'be grateful' list	A list of what and whom you should be grateful for in your life.	Chapter 8

Summary of chapters and key steps

Chapter 1 'T' – Time for you

While we are well aware of the things we *should* take time for for ourselves, we frequently fail to actually do it, don't we? This chapter covered how you need help to begin to empower yourself to be the person you want to be – need to be – and how to take small actions today to help create and begin to truly enjoy your life.

A reminder on how I personally broke through this

All I ask is that you do the first thing – book some time for yourself like it's the most important meeting of your life. Even if you can only spare an hour, take some time to yourself to reflect (and make sure you have some paper just in case. . .).

Step 1 – Take some
time for yourself

Step 2 – Write down
the first thing that
comes into your mind

Step 3 – Write down
what is missing from
your life currently

Step 4 – Analyse all
parts of your life in
detail

Step 5 – Give yourself
permission to look to
the future

Chapter 2 'A' – Address the past

This chapter encouraged you to 'unlearn' what you may believe about yourself, and begin to free yourself of your past by recognising where you have come from.

A reminder on how I personally broke through this

The main thing I realised was that I spent so much time worrying about what other people needed, I never gave any focus to figuring out what I need. I was always thinking, planning, coming up with new ideas, new schemes, doing new things, but I never paused and reflected on 'why' and 'where' I was going.

When I finally began to reflect on what had happened to me, my life and what I wanted to achieve, it was the first time I had ever really given myself the space, and the permission, to do so. The ten main areas in this text all began with that one idea, and the many things I go on to suggest have been how I began to work on myself, experiment on myself and refine my approach to life.

Step 1 – Create a timeline of your life to date

Step 2 – 'Own' your timeline

Step 3 – Create a new future timeline of where you want to be

Step 4 – Embrace how the future makes you feel

Chapter 3 'R' – Reboot yourself

This chapter encouraged you to really begin progressing by developing a new persona – your 'target self' – an authentic vision of where you are trying to get to in the future.

A reminder on how I personally broke through this

My main realisation, when performing the steps in the diagram, was how little I had actually given myself permission to admit that I was not perfect, I did not know all of the answers, and that I needed help – another person to talk to instead of just talking to myself.

If you've done everything I've suggested, you will now have said out loud: 'it is okay that I don't know all of the answers, and can't do this all myself'.

Step 1 – When thinking of your 'target self', think of who you are – start the sentence with 'I am...'

Step 2 – Think of what you have – start the sentence with 'Through hard work, I am lucky to have...'

Step 3 – Think of what you give to others – start the sentence with 'I am able to give...'

Step 4 – Think of whom you have with you – start the sentence with 'Around me I have...'

Chapter 4 'G' – Gain knowledge

This chapter focused on developing new core strengths and capabilities through acquiring new knowledge and skills. We explored how to unlock some ideas and find out if you are suited to a different learning style that might help you learn in a more structured and meaningful way. There is so much great content and learning material out there to use in your journey – so get out there and start taking it in! Remember, choose the steps below that make sense for your preferred learning style – you don't need to do all of them!

A reminder on how I personally broke through this

For me, gaining an appreciation of how different learning styles affect the way I take in information was a game-changer. As I began to explore the massive amount of interesting and inspiring content available, I also began to be more open in terms of my mind and heart to new ideas, more complex thinking and differing perspectives to my own. Now I treat every day as a learning experience – and there is always something new to discover.

Step 1 – Download an app like YouTube to your phone and search for themes from this book that are of interest.

Step 2 – Search for podcasts on your smartphone and save some episodes to listen to.

Step 3 – Buy three new books on an area that has interested you in this book.

Step 4 – Try out different learning styles to see what works for you.

Step 5 – Make a conscious effort to *really* listen during conversations.

Chapter 5 'E' – Energy sources

This chapter addressed the need for you to find help through positive 'energy sources' from people and experiences, and to (critically) learn to avoid negative impacts on your life – encouraging you to find the more positive aspects of life to keep you going through this journey.

A reminder on how I personally broke through this

My main take out from doing this myself was becoming far more aware of how certain people affected me, both positively and negatively – my major breakthrough here was to proactively schedule family and friends time, and to turn off my phone while I was with them. I can't tell you the difference it makes, so please do try it. Please also try to book some time to help yourself if you've been putting off – a physiotherapist, an osteopath, a massage therapist, visiting the doctor – just do it today.

Step 1 – Where do you see your priorities in terms of balancing your energy sources?

Step 2 – Really reflect on your friendships and how much they bring positive energy to you and support your goals

Step 3 – Prioritise family time, especially with those you like!

Step 4 – Exercise is key: schedule to do three to five sessions a week

Step 5 – Plan and execute a healthy sleep routine

Step 6 – Me time: have some!

Chapter 6 'T' – Targets for this year

This chapter introduced the idea of putting down some markers for the next year, or a shorter period of time, where you can actively control what happens and focus on some really meaningful progress. This chapter also covered my 'SIMPLE' framework, to ensure that you can set effective objectives that are well-constructed, measurable and, uniquely, have a return on investment.

A reminder on how I personally broke through this

Once I had actually invested the time in pulling together a list of more granular things that I wanted to achieve, I also began to feel so much clearer on my day-to-day priorities. So, using your future 'target self' vision, now ask yourself – 'where do I want to be in a year's time?'. Remember to try to enjoy the challenge, don't fear it – but push it and see what you can make happen.

Step 1 – Give yourself some space to consider what you want to have achieved by this time next year

Step 2 – Create a list of four to eight specific things you want to have 'done' by the end of the next year

Step 3 – Review your list and ensure your objectives meet all parts of the 'SIMPLE' formula

Step 4 – Consider if you have too many objectives

Step 5 – What are your priorities?

Chapter 7 'S' – Sidetrackers

This chapter focused on recognising, removing where possible, or at least reducing what I call 'sidetrackers'. Typically, these are things that are blocking your progress on something – distractions that get in the way or be sources of real daily pain. We explored a variety of approaches to tackling these so that they don't get in the way of you achieving your targets.

A reminder on how I personally broke through this

The game-changer for me in all of this was actually taking a minute to reflect on why I was feeling the way I was in any given moment. Capturing and managing these really freed up a lot of spare processing capacity in my brain, as I didn't need to think about them so much – I could just recognise them, be okay with them and move on.

Step 1 – Write down some of the times you've felt strong feelings about emotions, finances or people 'stopping you' doing something

Step 2 – Try the 5-Second Rule

Step 3 – Reflect on day-to-day blockers – what stopped you doing what you needed to do yesterday? Capture a list to spot any patterns

Step 4 – Create your list of known 'splinters' – things that block you – so you 'own' them, not them owning you

Step 5 – Review your 'target self' personal vision. Review the progress you've made so far in achieving your Target Self

Chapter 8 'E' – Everyday routines

This chapter focused on practical ways you can implement new structures in your everyday routines – for example, in the morning and evening lists – in order to further focus on removing the sources of daily pain, focusing on removing a key blocker for most people, which is a lack of preparedness, and instead concentrating on reflection, addressing journalling, meditation and how you speak to yourself – both positively and negatively.

A reminder on how I personally broke through this

Introducing the concept of a mini daily stand-up, where I go through my coming day and reflect on what I achieved yesterday, has become essential to my daily life now. Also, I can't tell you the difference having a clear 'walk out the door list' of things I am likely to need that day has made to reducing my daily stress levels!

Step 1 – Support your journey through daily visualisation of achieving your 'target self' personal vision

Step 2 – Create a daily routine that is yours, but keep to it – every single day

Step 3 – Create a reflection list, with 'themes' for how you want to be this year

Step 4 – Do you have a prioritised to-do list of the one, three or five things you need to do at any one time?

Step 5 – Learn to love positive thoughts and to laugh at negative ones

Chapter 9 'L' – Less is more

This chapter focused on being more ruthless with your time. There are so many distractions in life – from people, devices, advice to things that seem positive, but may derail you. We discussed some inspiration and suggestions to prioritise ruthlessly to ensure your goals, strategies and projects deliver, and have a meaningful impact in achieving your 'target self'.

A reminder on how I personally broke through this

Wow, saying 'no' is so massively hard – and the sooner I tackled it the better things were for me. I began to try to practise saying 'no', and it is interesting to realise how many times a day people and things come up that can derail you from what you are focusing on. So, learn to test saying 'no' – but remember to be nice! Once you've mastered that, open up your mind by also occasionally saying 'yes' when you normally wouldn't, in order to counterbalance things.

Step 1 – Create a 'next year' list for any objectives that you don't want to 'swap' for equivalent ones in this year

Step 2 – Become aware of being distracted and build these distractions into a list you can refer to

Step 3 – Test saying 'no' five times this week

Step 4 – Test saying 'yes' to one thing you would ordinarily say 'no' to

Step 5 – If you are not sure, it is okay to say so, and to ask for more information

Chapter 10 'F' – Focus and failure

This chapter looked at one of the hardest parts of self-motivation – focusing on developing sustained momentum while also embracing, and then handling, failure. It explored how key to this is a 'test and learn' approach, and using lessons to provide continued and renewed focus to develop sustained momentum and also a greater understanding of yourself.

A reminder on how I personally broke through this

My main realisation from this work was how little I had given myself permission to fail, or to be comfortable with the notion that I cannot get everything right first time and that I am not perfect, basically! The sooner I embraced the fact I did not know all of the answers, and that I needed to learn through doing and also seeking the help of other people, the sooner I made massive, massive progress.

So, if you've done everything I've suggested, you will now have said out loud: 'it is okay that I don't know all of the answers, and can't do this all myself'.

Thanks again for reading this book, it really means so much to me. For more information, tools and advice, go to www. drgeraintevans.com

Step 1 – Start (or end if you prefer) with a review of your day and what you are looking to achieve next.

Step 2 – Adopt a 'test and learn' mentality when progressing your objectives.

Step 3 – Decide on how far ahead you want to plan in terms of your next set of tasks.

Step 4 – Try to ensure you focus 100% on your current task.

Step 5 – Try to focus on only a few urgent/important tasks each day.

Step 6 – Consider approaching a mentor for coaching.

Step 7 – Consider telling someone you trust about your new goals for more support.

Further reading

If you want to dive into some of the content in this text in more detail, here are some other books in this space that can act as jumping-off points for different concepts I've covered, or for additional inspiration if you have found this motivating. (And, good news, if you look at even one of these and buy it/read it, then remember you are already taking action and learning!)

Achor, Shawn, *The Happiness Advantage: The Seven Principles of Positive Psychology That Fuel Success and Performance at Work*

Altucher, James, *Choose Yourself! Be Happy, Make Millions, Live the Dream*

Banayan, Alex, *The Third Door: The Wild Quest to Uncover How the World's Most Successful People Launched Their Careers*

Beck, Martha, *Finding Your Own North Star: How to Claim the Life You Were Meant to Live*

Beck, Martha, *The Joy Diet: 10 Steps to a Happier Life*

Bernstein, Gabrielle, *The Universe Has Your Back: How to Feel Safe and Trust Your Life No Matter What*

Brach, Tara, *Radical Acceptance: Awakening the Love that Heals Fear and Shame Within Us*

Brower, Elena, *Practice You: A Journal*

Brown, Brené, *Daring Greatly: How the Courage to Be Vulnerable Transforms the Way We Live, Love, Parent and Lead*

Buckingham, Marcus and Clifton, Donald, *Now, Discover Your Strengths*

Carlson, Richard, *Don't Sweat the Small Stuff and It's All Small Stuff: Simple Ways to Keep the Little Things From Taking Over Your Life*

Carnegie, Dale, *How to Win Friends and Influence People*

Downs, Annie, *100 Days to Brave: Devotions for Unlocking Your Most Courageous Self*

Duarte, Nancy and Sanchez, Patti, *Illuminate: Ignite Change Through Speeches, Stories, Ceremonies, and Symbols*

Duckworth, Angela, *Grit: The Power of Passion And Perseverance*

Duhigg, Charles, *Smarter, Faster, Better: The Secrets Of Being Productive*

Dweck, Carol, *Mindset: Changing the Way You Think to Fulfil Your Potential*

Ferriss, Tim, *Tools of Titans: The Tactics, Routines and Habits of Billionaires, Icons and World-Class Performers*

Ferriss, Timothy, *The 4-Hour Work Week: Escape the 9–5, Live Anywhere and Join the New Rich*

Forleo, Marie, *Everything is Figureoutable*

Heath, Chip and Dan, *Switch: How to Change Things When Change is Hard*

Heller, Cathy, *Don't Keep Your Day Job: How to Turn Your Passion Into Your Career*

Herman, Todd, *The Alter Ego Effect: The Power of Secret Identities to Transform Your Life*

Hill, Napoleon, *Think And Grow Rich*

Howes, Lewis, *The School of Greatness: A Real-World Guide To Living Bigger, Loving Deeper, And Leaving a Legacy*

John, Daymond, *The Power of Broke: How Empty Pockets, a Tight Budget, and a Hunger for Success Can Become Your Greatest Competitive Advantage*

Kshirsagar, Suhas, *Change Your Schedule, Change Your Life: How to Harness the Power of Clock Genes to Lose Weight, Optimize Your Workout, and Finally Get a Good Night's Sleep*

Manson, Mark, *The Subtle Art of Not Giving A F*Ck: A Counterintuitive Approach to Living a Good Life*

Millington, Caroline, *The Friendship Formula: Add Great Friends, Subtract Toxic People and Multiply Your Happiness*

Mylett, Ed, *#MAXOUT Your Life: Strategies for Becoming an Elite Performer*

Patel, Neil, Vlaskovits, Patrick and Koffler, Jonas, *Hustle: The Power to Charge Your Life with Money, Meaning, and Momentum*

Peale, Norman Vincent, *The Power of Positive Thinking*

Pink, Daniel, *When: The Scientific Secrets of Perfect Timing*

Rampolla, Mark, *High-Hanging Fruit: Build Something Great by Going Where No One Else Will*

Rhimes, Shonda, *Year of Yes: How to Dance It Out, Stand in the Sun and Be Your Own Person*

Robbins, Anthony, *Awaken the Giant Within: How to Take Immediate Control of Your Mental, Emotional, Physical and Financial Destiny*

Robbins, Mel, *The 5 Second Rule: Transform Your Life, Work, And Confidence With Everyday Courage*

Schwartz, David, *The Magic of Thinking Big*

Scott, Steve and Davenport, Barrie, *Declutter Your Mind: How to Stop Worrying, Relieve Anxiety, and Eliminate Negative Thinking*

Scott, Steve and Davenport, Barrie, *The Mindfulness Journal: Daily Practices, Writing Prompts, and Reflections for Living in the Present Moment*

Sincero, Jen, *You Are A Badass: How to Stop Doubting Your Greatness and Start Living an Awesome Life*

Tapper, Alice Paul, *Raise Your Hand*

Tracy, Brian, *Eat That Frog! Get More of the Important Things Done Today*

Tracy, Brian, *No Excuses! The Power of Self-Discipline*

Van der Kolk, Bessel, *The Body Keeps the Score: Mind, Brain and Body in the Transformation of Trauma*

Vaynerchuck, Gary, *The Thank You Economy*

Ware, Bronnie, *The Top Five Regrets of the Dying: A Life Transformed by the Dearly Departing*

Willink, Jocko and Babin, Leif, *Extreme Ownership: How U.S. Navy Seals Lead and Win*

Index